MW00562801

Out of Hiding

Finding the Courage to Be Me

JUDY JAMES

OUT OF HIDING
Finding the Courage to Be Me

Copyright © 2021. Judy James.

All rights reserved. No part of this publication may be reproduced, distributed, or transmitted in any form or by any means, including photocopying, recording, or other electronic or mechanical methods, without the prior written permission of the copyright holder, except in the case of brief quotations embodied in critical reviews and certain other noncommercial uses permitted by copyright law.

Cover and Interior Design by Transcendent Publishing
www.transcendentpublishing.com

Author Photo Credit: Keith Borgmeyer

ISBN: 978-0-578-30868-5

Printed in the United States of America.

Dedication

To my mom and my husband Clint, the two people who taught me
how to truly love myself.

Tammy!
   Thanks so much for
all your loving Support!
I appreciate YOU!

♡ Judy

Contents

Introduction

"If you're brave enough to leave behind everything familiar and comforting and set out on a truth-seeking journey, either internally or externally. And if you are willing to regard everything on that journey as a clue. If you accept everyone you meet along the way as a teacher, and if you are prepared, most of all, to face and forgive some very difficult things about yourself, then the truth will not be withheld from you."

This is my favorite passage from a book I love, *by Elizabeth Gilbert, Eat, Pray, Love,* not just for its profound message but because it so perfectly describes the course I set out on in my forties. Indeed, mine has been an internal journey, one of questioning everything I thought I knew about myself and my life. As I opened up to a greater knowing, I discovered that weaved through everyone I meet and every experience I have are clues to my true essence. All I had to do is be open to it all, especially the part about forgiving myself.

The Journey

*O*ut of Hiding: Finding the Courage to Be ME was placed in my heart to help me heal. I started this journey a couple of years ago with only thoughts of myself and what I needed. I didn't have anyone else in mind. Even now, saying that sounds selfish, and that's fine. You see, I had always thought being selfish was something bad and only people who didn't care about others were selfish. Along the way, however, I've found that being selfish is not only a good thing but it's necessary to live my best life.

Growing up, I was taught that I came first… right after everyone else had what they needed. I don't remember anyone actually saying that, it's just what I saw my mom do. And, like Mom, I've always been very sensitive and wanted to please everyone so their lives would be easier. It was natural for me to put my needs last. I didn't even know I was doing it. I just knew that a "good girl" would take care of everyone else and make do with whatever time and energy she had left. By the way, most times others didn't ask me to take on their emotions, worry for them, and try to solve all their issues; in fact, they didn't even realize that that's what I was doing. I just took it upon myself to do and be everything for everybody. And, despite the lack of appreciation I often received for my efforts, this worked for me. I felt needed, plus it kept me so busy "fixing" everyone else I didn't even have time to think about fixing myself.

Then came the point when it just didn't work for me anymore. I began to become bitter, resentful, and overwhelmed with all I had taken on. If anyone asked me for something I would fly off the handle. I became a "yeller," taking my frustrations out on my family and others closest to me. Of course, they had no idea what was going on inside me, why I was acting so differently. I, on the other hand, was sure they knew.

How could they not see that I was constantly thinking about what they should do and how they should fix their problems? It became unbearable. *Why wouldn't they just stop?*

One day someone asked me, "What do you like?" Just a simple question, right? Wrong. It was one of those moments so profound it felt like time stopped. I was in my mid-forties at the time. I was married, had four kids, two businesses, the house, the car, great vacations, everything anyone could want. So why did those four little words make my eyes well up with tears? Not knowing what to do with this wave of emotion, I quickly dismissed the question with a sarcastic comment and a laugh. It was what I always did when something made me feel exposed. Just so you know, I was the only girl growing up with five brothers, so there was no such thing as vulnerability. I buried my feelings deep. No one was ever going to see this girl cry; that was the ultimate sign of weakness in my mind. But later that night, after I had marked all the things off my "to-do list" for the day, I lay in the silence of my dark bedroom, thought about that question, and let the tears come. I couldn't think of anything I liked. I felt defeated and alone. I remember looking up and saying, "I don't know what to do. For the first time in my life, I don't know what to do."

That very moment, my life started to change. If it had been the scene in a movie the heavens would have opened with a beam of golden white light streaming down on my head; my arms would have been out-stretched and there would have been angels singing in the background with full, white flowing robes with shiny golden halos on their heads of beautiful curly hair. Have you ever had a moment like that? It's only looking back that it was like that; it didn't seem that way at the time. I didn't know it then, but what I did in that dark bedroom was surrender. Now, I didn't say *give up,* I said *surrender* – two very different things. Giving up would have meant I quit right where I was. Surrender meant that I would release the resistance I had to growing and expanding into the ME I truly wanted. I had outgrown my comfortable, very small world where I knew everything. I had learned manipulation and used it to get what I wanted with ease. And I became so uncomfortable in my longing for something more that I had to find what was missing.

I can tell you now that what was missing was ME. I didn't know who I was. I was hiding behind who I thought I should be, who I thought others thought I should be, and the fear of finding out that I might be something else entirely. Maybe the biggest thing I was hiding from was my greatness. We are all born with our own greatness. We start hiding it for a lot of reasons. We believe what others say about us, we want to fit in and have friends, or maybe we want to make someone else feel better.

I wrote this book to honor my journey back to ME. Each layer I peel back reveals more of who I am and who I always was. Everything I write reveals more of the treasure I have locked away. This will be a lifelong process. We always have more to learn about ourselves.

I know for sure that the process of learning about myself has brought me freedom. I realized that I had given my power away and I was responsible for taking it back. That's not always easy, and I've met with plenty of resistance. Even though people hadn't asked me to put their needs before mine, they had become accustomed to it. People don't like change, but if they really love you, they will respect your boundaries. I had to be okay finding out who loved me and who loved what I did for them.

This sacred journey of transformation is available to anyone who longs for more meaning in their life and is brave enough to leave the comfort of what they know behind. Anyone who is willing to face and forgive some very difficult realities about themselves. Anyone with the courage to surrender to their truest self.

In the following pages you will read about some of the things, both internal and external, painful and joyful, that I have experienced during my journey. It is my hope that they encourage and inspire you as you undergo your own transformation, and, most importantly, let you know you are never, ever alone.

Many of the sections in this book begin with a quote. Some are from thought leaders and spiritual teachers; others are truths I realized along the way. I encourage you to breathe into them, use them as affirmations, and see the healing magic these words can work in your life.

The truest, most gratifying life I can imagine is one where I freely express who I am without fear of judgment, especially from myself. I give myself permission to be ME. That is my greatest privilege and the best gift of my life. It can be yours too. Try it, you'll see!

The Wall

When did it all change for you?

Do you remember the exact moment? The moment you put yourself – that beautiful, brilliant, carefree, vibrant, all-knowing little girl inside you – behind glass?

A glass so thick that no one could hear or understand what you were really saying? The glass that hid your feelings so you looked good, looked "together," no matter what?

Sure, people could still see the outer you, but they couldn't get close to the real you inside. Did it happen all at once, or little by little? Did you go willingly, or did you kick and scream all the way?

I don't remember a lot about my early childhood. But I do remember the day I handed the sweet, blond-haired, hazel-eyed little girl within me over.

I was at my maternal grandparents' house, where I was left sometimes to "babysit" them because they were alcoholics. I guess Mom always thought she could fix them, so she started training me to do the same.

I don't recall what happened that day, I just remember my grandpa "sleeping" on the faded orange couch in the entryway of their house… my mom taking me into the kitchen. We were standing by the buffet that held my grandma's pretty dishes.

I can still see her looking down at me with such desperation that I knew she was about to break wide open. I could feel her pain radiating through my body as if it were my own. There were no tears – they weren't really allowed – only desperation.

I somehow knew, at four years old, that Mom couldn't handle this. And somehow I knew *I* could. And I knew she knew I could. And so I did.

At four years old I vowed to never tell…to keep this secret…to never speak of it to anyone.

You see…

My mom was the protector of her parents and siblings, and now I was *her* protector.

It was now top priority for me to take on everything that my mom couldn't handle.

This was all unspoken, of course. My mom would NEVER have knowingly placed such a burden on me.

And she never HAD to…I looked for every opportunity to take on everything even before she knew she couldn't handle it.

She already had so much on her plate. By this time, she'd had four kids in five years – I was the only girl. There would be two more boys, born eight and twelve years later. My dad was totally occupied with working full-time and farming full-time, so the motherload fell on me. And I took it on.

I remember when I was little doing things just so my mom would notice and be happy.

I would clean the house and lock my brothers out. I always told myself it was because I wanted it to stay clean, but really, I just wanted Mom's praise.

It's only over the past few years that I started unraveling the tight web of manipulation I was caught in.

My self-realization was zero…I felt invisible, so I thought my words and actions didn't matter. I didn't know why; I didn't even know to question why.

I had no idea that I wasn't thinking for myself or daring to dream of what life could be. That would have been like telling God that what I had wasn't good enough.

What did you have to do as a child to feel loved?

I asked my husband that question. I thought it was a normal one, so I was baffled when he turned to me with a look of total disbelief. It was his words, though, that really threw me:

"What do you mean…Why would I have to do something, what would I do? I don't understand…I just always knew I was very loved."

That was a big realization for me. I thought everyone grew up in a "normal" home like mine.

I mean, it was so much better than how my mom grew up. Didn't that make it "normal"?

My parents weren't drunks that couldn't pay their bills…we always had a roof over our heads, clothes, and food. So we were good, right? What more was there?

One thing there was always more of was hard work. That was life on a farm, and it was ingrained in me. I liked working hard; I liked giving it my all.

Hard work was a great distraction from thinking about what I wanted. I didn't deserve to have what I wanted until the work was done, and the work was never done.

My hardest "job" was to make my mom feel better. If she could feel better, she could be happy, and if she could be happy, she could love herself, and if she could love herself, I would have done a good job and I could be proud and happy and…

MAYBE, I COULD FINALLY BE WORTHY OF LOVE.

That would be my permission.

I never got that permission when my mom was alive.

I always felt my greatness. My mom did too, I could tell, but it frightened her because she knew she had greatness too… hidden, waiting to be seen. If she acknowledged my greatness, she would have to admit to hers too, and she was either unable or unwilling to do that. It was easier to use her greatness for everyone else, so that's what she did. She did everything for everyone else.

My mom was so afraid of this greatness that she took it with her…

Over the years, I had pounded on the glass wall I was trapped behind. I was screaming in frustration, but I never expressed what was truly going on, that I was dying inside.

Instead, it would come out because someone made a mess or didn't do what I thought they should do. I was defensive and unhappy, always looking for what was wrong instead of what was right.

Always waiting for the other shoe to drop.

I spent most of my life not knowing I could just step out from behind that wall. I didn't know that if I stopped yelling and simply but firmly spoke my truth, people would hear me. I didn't know that some people would even relate and find the courage to be vulnerable enough to let their own greatness shine.

A few years after Mom passed, she came to me. I'll get into the details of that experience later; suffice it to say I felt her presence and heard her whisper words that radiated with a love I had never felt from her when she was in physical form. Those words would change my life forever.

I did it for you, she said, *I did it FOR YOU.*

Everything I thought I knew about myself and my life changed at that moment.

I had thought I was saving her. I had thought I was loving her so she would love herself...

Could it be that our greatest challenges can show us what we need to know about ourselves so we can heal?

Could it be that she was shining a light on something that would change my life, not hers?

Could it be that my mom didn't even know what I was doing for her all those years?

WHAT IF...

What if my mom had used all her greatness for me? What if everything she did was to teach me to love myself and live the life I wanted... to choose me?

What if she poured me full of greatness so I could come out on the other side and show my greatness without apology?

What if what she did gave me the opportunity to break through and show others how to do the same?

What if I looked at it all from a higher perspective?

What if... I could have known this when she was alive?

How different would things have been?

What if I wasn't supposed to know back then?

What if everything had worked out just like it needed to?

What if I couldn't have gained the strength, courage, vulnerability, and wisdom I came here to share in any other way?

What if I did start sharing what I had learned?

Then my mom's greatness will shine through me.

Acceptance

The real difficulty is to overcome how you think about yourself.

– Maya Angelou

The Choice

"I think kind, loving thoughts about myself and others."

We all have parts of ourselves that we are unaware of. We can unknowingly pile layers of expectations on ourselves, then mete out punishment when we don't live up to them. Having a critical inner voice was one way I did that.

This voice has been a part of me ever since I can remember. I don't know where it came from or why it started, and I often think I must have been born with it. The words played over and over in my head for so long that I wasn't aware of them: "You're stupid"; "You're not smart enough... not pretty enough... not rich enough"; and on and on. Even on the rare occasion I thought I did something well, critical thoughts would creep in comparing what I did or had to someone else. I felt like I could never measure up.

I am a recovering perfectionist. I always wanted everything to be perfect, or, more accurately, it had to look perfect from the outside. I didn't pay too much attention to the inside. That's how I lived most of my life. As long as everything looked perfect on the outside, then it was good. I hid a lot behind new clothes and shoes and a clean house. If I appeared to have it all together then I must have it all together, right? That's what I thought anyway.

On some level, I believed that everyone had a critical inner voice shaming and blaming them. Isn't that what pushed them to get things done? Didn't everyone's critical voice force them to handle what life dealt them? That's what mine did. It was the drive behind my pursuit of perfection.

I forced myself to show up and do what I thought I "should," yet nothing was good enough. I never gave myself a pat on the back or

3

said, "Good job." Instead, I picked everything apart. Even when others told me I had accomplished something great, I would deflect the compliment by telling them everything I wished I had done better. I never let myself win or celebrate my accomplishments. Before long I was on to the next item on my to-do list. I would try again. Maybe this time I could get it right.

This pattern was so deeply ingrained that I didn't even realize it was there; feeling like I was not enough was simply the norm. It also had led to my insecurity and people-pleasing. If I could just impress them, then maybe, just maybe, I could be worthy.

My path from self-criticism to self-love has not been all hearts and flowers. It has at times been painful and has shown me what I don't want to be. It has also shown me how different life can be when we choose to look for the good in everything. As I have quieted my critical voice, I find I have compassion and empathy for myself. I get to celebrate my wins! I get to receive the benefits of my accomplishments! Allowing myself to receive has also allowed me to be supportive of others. I am no longer critical of them; instead, I extend compassion and empathy knowing we are all doing the very best that we can in every moment.

Being a hairstylist for forty years has taught me a lot about my critical voice. Success in the beauty industry is dependent upon making people happy. There are few times I remember thinking my work was perfect. No matter how much praise I got, there was always something I could have done better. Now, there is always more to learn, and striving to do better is how we grow; that is much different, however, than constantly berating yourself with critical comments. Striving to do better is about lifting yourself up; it's never about tearing yourself down.

I want to share one of my favorite stories from behind the chair. To say this encounter had an impact on me is an understatement. It changed me and opened me up to possibilities I hadn't allowed myself to consider. It made me realize how my critical voice had kept me from experiencing the connection I longed for.

Grace is eighty-eight years young with fiery curly red hair that matches her temperament. When she came to the salon, she was new to the area and apprehensive about leaving her stylist of many years. From the first time I did her hair she loved it, and when she returned the next week, it looked just as good as when she had left. She was so happy she made a standing weekly appointment, which would have been great except for one thing. Grace spent the entire thirty minutes – longer when she got a cut and a color – talking about her hair – "It's too curly"; "It's too frizzy"; "It's not shiny," and so on. For weeks and months, she would show up each Friday morning at nine-thirty and immediately launch into the litany of complaints about her hair. She never complained about my work; in fact, she continued to be very complimentary, even saying that no one had ever made her hair look the way I did. In time, I got really tired of hearing about her hair and I became annoyed with her. I started to dread Friday mornings. Not only was I critical of myself, I was critical of others too. I chose to see the negative, it was familiar to me.

All that changed one day when I finished with Grace's style. Until that point it had been no different than every other Friday, with Grace criticizing her hair from the minute she sat in the chair. This day however, as she looked in the mirror, tears welled up in her eyes. "Thank you so much for taking such good care of my hair," she said, "it always looks so beautiful when you style it." I looked at her, surprised by the emotion in her voice. I told her it was my pleasure. She continued, "You know, my hair is my most redeeming quality; it's all I've really ever had going for me."

I fought back tears as I walked Grace to the lobby. I had gotten an insight into what was behind her critical voice; I also realized that although my critical voice was internal, the pain of not feeling good enough was the same. The fear of rejection for what we thought was not perfect in us was the same. I got a lesson in love and acceptance that day. I learned to accept Grace exactly as she is and, by extension, to accept myself exactly how I am as well. That was the beginning of quieting my critical voice. With some reflection I came to understand that my annoyance with Grace was there to teach me to look at myself. I am happy to report that I look forward to seeing Grace every Friday morning. Believe me, Grace has not changed, but she didn't need to. I did.

We long for connection. We want to be accepted. I think I formed my critical voice to keep me safe. That probably sounds counterintuitive, considering the amount of damage it has done, but it's true. What it kept me safe from is rejection. I rejected myself every day because I couldn't bear the pain of someone else doing it. Being critical of self and others somehow tricked me into thinking I did not want connection.

Even after that epiphany with Grace, it took a while to quiet my mean girl voice. There are still times when she resurfaces with a vengeance. The difference is I now know to talk nice to her and let her know I'm safe and can handle things myself. It's taken a lot of work, patience, and self-love to get to this point, but it has made my life much sweeter. It has made me much lighter.

Be inspired:

I have learned that accepting myself where I am quiets my critical voice and allows me to grow in love for myself and others.

Journal Prompt:

Make a list of your critical thoughts in the left column.

Challenge each one of those thoughts in the column on the right.

Ask yourself if what you thought is true.

Ask yourself what you will choose to see in the situation.

The Gifts

If you focus on the hurt, you will continue to suffer. If you focus on the lesson, you will continue to grow."

– Buddha

Many of our earliest teachings come from our parents. They teach us by telling us what to do and how to be. I believe that even more is learned by watching what they do. It is not only in the watching, but in the perceiving; it is what we tell ourselves about it that matters. What if our "work" as adults is to unwind those stories and see what is true for us now?

Blessings From My Earliest Teachings

As you have probably guessed by now, one of my greatest teachers in this life has been my mom. She was a strong woman who could handle everything, including everyone else's problems. She was always giving advice to family and friends. She tirelessly gardened and canned food in the summer for the winter. She volunteered at church and school. She did laundry, cooked, and cleaned for eight people. We all worked hard, but my mom was the one that kept everything going. She took care of everyone, except herself.

I believe that some of us are born to take care of others. I believe that is a beautiful thing. Sometimes it's passed on from generation to generation. We watched what our moms did and we do the same.

I spent most of my life doing what my mom did. I admired her and thought she had all the answers. She taught me so many things that I still hold dear. She always said, "You never know what someone is going through so give them the benefit of the doubt." She was kind to strangers. She was always there for her friends and family. She loved making people feel welcome. After she passed, my dad laughed and said, "Your mother always made a point to welcome anyone new at church after mass was over. Hell, I never paid much attention to who was there." He seemed proud that she did that. I was a mixture of both of them. I paid attention to who was there but I never put myself out there to introduce myself to them.

As the only girl I was expected to be perfect, and I took that job very seriously. I learned to cook, clean, do laundry and all the things that a "good girl" did. I learned to take care of everyone and everything and, as I mentioned earlier, I really didn't mind. It made me feel like I was important. It made me feel like what I did mattered, so I mattered. I looked incessantly for what I could do next for someone else.

The problem with all of this is that I was totally dependent on others for my value. As long as I was pleasing them, life was good. There were a lot of good times, but they often came at the expense of my own desires. I sometimes wonder where I would be today if I had put all the energy that I put into others into myself.

As mentioned, I designated myself as my mom's keeper, just as she had been the keeper of her own mother. I told myself that I could handle what she couldn't. That wasn't true. What was true is that it was easier for me to take things on myself than to watch her be sad or angry or struggling. This is because I am a "feeler," or empath. I am very sensitive to the energy of others. I didn't understand all this until just a few years ago and I'm learning more about it all the time.

No one knew what I was doing – how could they, when I didn't even know it myself. I just took on everything in silence. I would observe Mom being sad about something and I would be sad. I wouldn't even know what she was sad about, I could just feel her sadness. If I asked what was wrong, she would always say, "Nothing, I'm fine." I know she was trying to protect me from knowing things that kids didn't need to know. But what was actually happening was that I was feeling her emotion and being told it wasn't true. That led to the confusion and self-doubt that would plague me for much of my life. I didn't feel safe anywhere or with anyone, so I hid deeper and deeper within myself.

Let me ask you this: When you have conversations with someone who is struggling do you feel what they are feeling? Do they often leave the conversation feeling better while you feel heavy and drained? If so, you may be taking on emotions and energy that are not yours.

I truly believe we choose our parents so we can learn what we came here to learn for our soul's growth and expansion. Now, I realize not everyone will agree with that. It's hard to imagine why someone would pick abusive parents or parents with addictions or parents who didn't show them love. Sometimes we choose parents who show us what we don't want for our lives. That can be the perfect motivation for being and creating what we do want.

My mom taught me both what I wanted to be and what I didn't want to be. She was just living the life she knew to live and I was learning how to live mine. I got some of my greatest qualities from my mom and some of my greatest struggles. I'm sure she could say the same about her own mother, and so on, through the generations.

It's a natural progression for an empath to move into enabling. It was for my mom and has been for me too. We both enabled many people by taking on their pain and not holding them accountable for their actions. We would make excuses for them and their behaviors continued. My mom continued this until she passed on, until she couldn't take anymore. I'm thankful that my own "couldn't take it anymore" came before that. My mom did what she knew to do and taught me to do something different.

One of the greatest lessons I learned from Mom is that being a victim is a choice. No matter what happens, we do not have to live our lives in powerlessness. The power to create the life we desire has always been within us. We just have to go after it, knowing we deserve it. I haven't always thought I deserved to have the life I wanted. I do now, thanks to my mom.

Many of my earliest teachings were unspoken. They were what I, as a very sensitive child, felt and embodied as what I was "supposed" to do. They were modeled to me by a mom who wanted me to be my best. My strong desire to make the world a better place was the drive behind taking on other's struggles and people-pleasing. Same with my mom. The problem with that is that *I* got lost in the process. I got so buried beneath what I took on that I forgot who I was and who I wanted to be.

Without my mom being who she was, I wouldn't be who I am. She too wanted to change the world and make it a better place. She did this by focusing on the little things, like gathering family and friends and cooking for them, and so do I. She also sent cards to everyone, not only for birthdays but just to let them know she was thinking about them (I'm not as good at that). Most importantly, she taught me to put myself first by not doing that for herself.

My mom was a remarkable woman. I am grateful for the life she gave me. Her greatness shines through me as I live free from what burdened her. I am blessed.

Be inspired:

I believe we all do the very best we can in every moment. Believing this frees me from judging myself and others. It allows me to be more compassionate.

Journal prompt:

Close your eyes. Quiet your mind. Trust that the memory that surfaces will hold a clue to unraveling a limited belief. Some of these memories seem insignificant until we look deeper.

Write about something you learned by watching what someone did, rather than what they said.

The Surrender

"All the possibilities of our life align in perfect Divine Time."

Most of my life I thought I had all the answers about how to get what I wanted. I knew how to make things happen. In other words, I was impatient and wanted what I wanted *now*. The only possibilities I could see were the ones I could make happen on my own. As a result, my dreams were small and dependent only on my ability to make them happen. This all changed when I learned to surrender.

When I looked at the date on my phone this morning I was reminded of the time in my life when I had the most upheaval I had ever experienced. It seems crazy to me that I could have been going through a major upheaval in my life yet still feel a sense of peace.

I got married when I was nineteen years old. I couldn't wait to be a grownup and live on my own. I married the first guy that came along because I thought I might not get another chance. Yep, at only nineteen I was sure that time was passing me by and I was going to miss something if I didn't force things to happen NOW. So I did. At the time and to the best of my ability to love, I loved him. I have to say here, that in my life then, love meant "fixing" someone and manipulating things to get my way.

He always had a good job and was financially responsible. He always went to work and paid his bills. He always hung out with his buddies and partied. It was rare for him to come home after work. He always had friends who needed something. I got used to it and thought everyone lived like that. I really didn't have any close friends. I know now that was because I was so closed off. I didn't allow anyone to get close. I couldn't possibly share what was going on in my life. How embarrassing that would be to admit that I was unhappy with the way things were. So I stuffed all those emotions down deep, hidden away.

Or so I thought.

I was filled with feelings of not being enough which led to self-loathing. I was sure to put on the perfect outfit and makeup and smile like everything was fine. I told myself so many times that it could be worse and that made it ok. I hid beneath the layers of working to get the next car or house or clothes or shoes or vacations. Keeping busy and working hard is how I measured my value. I thought everyone else did too. I worked tirelessly running my business and working and then did everything at home just so I could say how much I was doing. I desperately needed everyone to notice what I did and how perfect my life was. My validation was people saying 'I don't know how you do it, you're so busy. Your house is so clean and nothing is ever out of place. You look so nice'. These crumbs of attention kept me going for a long time. They filled me up. It didn't take much from the shallow place I was living.

That is, until those little praises stopped being enough to fill me up. I could no longer live in the shallow place I had created. I needed more in my life. What was missing that I so desperately wanted? I had no idea what would make me happy.

Admitting that I didn't know something was not easy for me. You see, from the small world I lived in at the time, I knew everything, I was sure of that. I always knew what to do next. I was strong and independent and didn't need anything from anyone. Admitting I needed help or didn't know what to do next meant weakness to me. It's interesting though, I didn't feel like that about anyone else, only me. I was understanding and compassionate towards anyone that needed it. I could extend grace to anyone except myself.

Desperate times call for desperate measures so I thought maybe I should pray about it. Praying meant I had to get quiet and listen for the answers and I didn't like to get quiet. Without all the outside noise, I had to listen to what was going on inside. It was time to realize some very difficult things about myself. I could no longer hide from my pain.

At that time praying and asking God for something was saved for desperate times. I thought I was supposed to struggle and try to figure things out on my own and only when I became totally exhausted could I dare ask for help. I thought we were meant to suffer before we could get our life together and be happy. Surely twenty-eight years in a marriage was long enough to figure it out on my own. I felt desperate and alone. My inner world was a train wreck and my outer world was starting to look the same way.

I had always asked for things to be resolved with the outcome I wanted. This time, I simply asked to be guided to the life I wanted to experience. Late one night I looked up and said, "For the first time in my life I don't know what to do. I've made a mess of things and I need help. I don't know what to do." I had been desperate and asked God for things before. This time was different.

This time I surrendered. I let go of control and learned to trust. I will tell you what happened after that I could never have orchestrated on my own. Opportunities and people magically appeared just when I needed them.

My life was filled with one miracle after another. Everything aligned in perfect order. A force that knows what is for my highest and greatest good took over. Every day I knew what to do. It was never a thought of 'maybe I should' instead it was a knowing that what came to my mind would lead me to the next, then the next thing I needed. One miracle after another presented itself and each led me with grace and ease through one of the most unknown times I had ever experienced. All I had to do was listen to my guidance and act on it. I had to trust. I had to let go of control and surrender.

There was a time when I didn't like the word surrender. I thought it meant you were weak and giving up. I have since learned that surrendering and giving up are very different. Surrender means 'to abandon oneself entirely to a powerful emotion or influence, to give into'. Surrendering is letting go of control. Giving up means 'ceasing to make an effort; to resign oneself to failure.' You stay stuck where you are and quit when you give up.

I will always see the night I surrendered as a turning point in my life. My Spirit had been patiently waiting for me to be ready to give up the constant struggle and live my best life. I'm sure my life was filled with miracles and synchronicities before my 'surrender'. I was just too busy to recognize and accept them. We see and experience what we are focused on. Putting our focus on one thing doesn't mean other things don't exist. It just means we are putting our focus on what we want. We are choosing and that is powerful.

Letting go of control and trusting our Guidance brings us abundant rewards. The Universe is quietly lining up everything our hearts desire. The only thing we have to do is get out of the way and allow the miracles and magic to happen. I have learned not to try to figure out how things will happen and just trust that they will. I have learned not to force things.

What I am sure of is that the Universe rarely delivers things the way I think they will be delivered.

Be inspired:

My life started to change when I began to release control of how I thought things were *supposed* to happen and be. I found that being in control was only an illusion. We're never really in control, and the harder we try to control things in our lives, the more exhausted we become. The only real control we have is how we show up in our own life.

Journal prompt:

Take a moment to close your eyes and put your hand on your heart. Think about surrender. How do you feel when you say 'surrender'? Write about what surrendering means to you.

Changes

Do the best you can until you know better.
Then when you know better, do better.

– Maya Angelou

The Obvious

"Oftentimes we don't see what's right in front of us."

When I was a little girl all I could think about was growing up. I didn't want to be where I was. I wanted to be able to decide for myself what I would do. School was a struggle too. I could make good grades without much effort, but I always felt trapped. I felt like I didn't belong. I didn't belong in my family, I didn't belong at church or at school, and that was pretty much all that was in my life back then. I had different ideas and never felt safe to express them. On the rare occasion that I did, I would be laughed at and asked where the idea had come from. Then I would be told the "truth" or the "right way" to think. I took all this in and day by day told myself that what I knew and felt was not true. I stopped trusting my own inner voice and listened to others. I started pouring my attention into others in the way of "helping" or "fixing." I placed my value in how others felt. If I could make them feel better, I would feel better.

I remember being young and fierce. That untamed part of me was the part that imagined all the beauty in the world and the magical places I would create and explore. I would often get lost in my daydreams for hours. I loved to pretend and make something out of nothing. My brothers and I used to play in an old chicken house on our farm. It hadn't been in use since my grandma and grandpa had chickens many years before, so I decided to turn it into a proper playhouse. From then on I spent all of my free time raking through the dirt floor and clearing it of chicken remnants. Any white feathers were collected to be used for decoration. I found bricks and boards and old cans and buckets to use in my house. I remember being frustrated that the brown dirt floor was not level, despite my raking the dirt to fill in the holes, but I kept going anyway. I worked so hard to make it beautiful. I learned to be resourceful, to use what I had and make the best of it. Looking back, it's a wonder we didn't get sick with some sort of bird disease; then again, maybe that's why I have such a strong immune system: all the exposure to "foreign" matter.

One day in particular stands out in my memory. I had worked for hours, carrying bricks and stacking them one by one, building a wall that was to be a grand entry to the playhouse. I had just finished putting the last brick down and stepped back to admire my work when one of my brothers appeared.

He looked at the wall and said, "Wow, that's cool," then he leaned on it and brought it tumbling down.

Without another word, he took off running. He knew I was going to be pissed, and I was. Anger was the only emotion that was acceptable in our house growing up. And if someone was angry, you'd better watch out! I took out after him but he managed to escape my wrath. I went back into my playhouse and sat in the middle of that pile of bricks. By that time the dust had cleared and I was starting to think how I would put my wall back up, or if I even would. If my brothers couldn't be more careful, why would I bother to do all that work again? But this feeling of defeat didn't last long, and soon I was at work rebuilding my wall.

That wall would get knocked down a hundred times (okay, maybe not that many, but it sure felt like that), and guess what? I got pissed off every time! When I started writing this, I had no idea where it was going. I just write what I'm guided to and trust it will make sense. I wasn't sure there was a moral to this story about building a wall again and again in a dirty old chicken house: but here it is: I kept doing something I knew would end badly. I didn't think I had a choice. I was so fixated on having that wall to make a grand entrance to my playhouse that I gave all my energy to fixing it.

When we keep doing the same thing over and over and expecting different results, we are setting ourselves up for disappointment. We are stuck in a cycle of giving our power away to the same experience or person. At that moment, I put my happiness in that wall standing. I put all my focus on only one way to make something work instead of being open to other options. It's a good thing we didn't have concrete mix or I would have fixed that wall good!

Those patterns followed me into adulthood, where there was "concrete," and plenty of it. I became so preoccupied with "fixing" others that there was no time for me. And while I may not have consciously realized it at the time, it was, on some level, intentional. I was uncomfortable looking at my own struggles so I looked at the struggles of others. This kept me so busy that I couldn't or wouldn't see what I needed to heal. I couldn't see other options.

Becoming aware that I was in a pattern I wanted to break, set the stage for transformation in myself and my life. It has taken years of disrupting these patterns in little ways for me to make the big changes I now see. These days, I spend my time working on my own life, and I trust that everyone is on their own journey and has everything they need to walk it. I can offer support *when asked*. I can walk with them without taking ON their challenges and emotions.

The cool thing is that the change in me ripples out to cause positive change in the world. This is one of the most important things I've learned. Changing the world is an inside job. It starts with a burning desire, an acknowledgment that we already have the power within us, and a willingness to shift and release thoughts and behaviors that have been holding us back.

Be inspired:

As I mentioned earlier, I am an empath, which makes it difficult for me to watch others have challenges. Back then, I actually thought I could fix them, which gave me a sense of purpose. They feel better and then I could feel better. It's a win-win, right? Actually, it was more like a lose-lose.

Because my self-worth was dependent on fixing them, when I couldn't, I would get angry and frustrated. Of course, it was *their* fault – mostly because they wouldn't listen and do what I thought they should do. At least that's what I told myself. The truth was I felt like a failure. I needed them to be better so I could give myself permission to feel better.

I wasn't doing the other person any favors either. People we love are going to struggle from time to time. Some people stay in struggle. It's all part of the lessons we're here to learn, and if I get too involved, they may not learn them. I could be taking away their opportunity to find the courage to do something they thought they couldn't do.

I have found that working on and healing myself is much more beneficial, not just for me but for everyone else. I take care of what I need to and inspire others to do the same. Our best support starts by lovingly staying in our own lane. I trust that we experience what we need to so we can become more of who we are.

Journal prompt:

How much time do you spend "fixing" others or situations that aren't yours to fix?

The Heart

*"Change is never painful, only the resistance
to change is painful."*

– Buddha

Learning to trust what my heart tells me instead of what my head tells me has been a process. I can tell when it is my heart speaking because it "feels" right, even when I think it doesn't make sense. I have learned to check in with how my body feels to tell the difference. Learning this has been life-changing for me.

I had always dreamed about being married. I wanted to share my life with someone who wanted to share theirs with me. I stayed in my first marriage twenty-eight years. It was all I knew. It seemed that for most people "for better or worse" meant settling for an unhappy or unfulfilling life. I assumed that everyone was like me and was just making the best of it.

Then the day came when I had no more excuses for behaviors, his or mine, and I chose to leave. It was a shock to everyone who knew us since we had been married for so long.

Shortly after the divorce was final a friend invited me to go to an event with her – a "girl's night out" to raise money for a charity she volunteered for. I spent all day getting ready, doing my hair and makeup and choosing the dress and heels I would wear. It was a rare occasion when I got to primp and I was going to savor every minute of it. I was also quite nervous, as I had been nineteen when I got married and barely even remembered being single. I also didn't love being social and doing the small talk thing; I just liked getting dressed up.

The event was lovely, and included some drawings for prizes and experiences. I entered a drawing to win a mini-session with a psychic, never dreaming I'd win. When my name was called, I was both excited and skeptical. I had always been fascinated with the spiritual world but wasn't sure I believed that someone could tell me about my future. I decided to be open to finding out and just enjoy.

When it was time for my session, I was led to a candlelit room with a small wooden table and two chairs. In the chair facing me was a woman with a pleasant smile. She invited me to sit in the open chair, then she introduced herself and said I could ask her three questions. The only restriction was that I couldn't ask about when I was going to die. I was good with that since I really didn't want to know.

"What's your first question?" she asked.

"When will I meet the love of my life, my soulmate?" That was my burning desire. I knew he was out there, looking for me, and though I was really happy being single I wanted to move on with my life. I wasn't getting any younger.

Almost before the words were out of my mouth, she replied, "Three years."

"Three years! Three years?" I thought that sounded like an extremely long time.

"You've been waiting a very long time, haven't you?"

"All my life."

She smiled. "You need to kick up your heels and have a good time! You've never done that! Because when he does walk into your life it will be like you are continuing your relationship from another lifetime, like you've known each other forever. Enjoy yourself now and be patient."

I don't recall the other two questions I asked that night. I only remember how I felt the truth of what I was told. He was out there; I just had to be patient. In the meantime, I would take the opportunity to just have fun and enjoy life. And that's what I did.

As time passed, however, I started thinking more and more about the soulmate I was waiting to meet. I thought about his kind, loving, caring heart. I thought about how generous he was and how accepting he was of me and my family. I felt what it would be like to be in his arms. I would feel safe, warm, protected and, most of all, loved. He would be the most loving person I had ever met.

I assumed that in addition to knowing about these wonderful attributes I also knew exactly how he would be. I was used to the rough-and-tumble type; the "bad boy"; the one who played it cool, showed no emotions. It never occurred to me that the Universe had someone so completely different lined up.

Clint and I met during my three-month trial on an online dating site – something I had reluctantly tried because I lived in a small town and am not very social. Indeed, I didn't like it at all, but I didn't feel like I had any other options. Clint was one of my matches, and he would email every couple of days asking how my day was and telling me a little about his. He taught fourth grade and always had good stories. He seemed nice enough. During my last week of online dating, he invited me to dinner that Saturday. He was helping his daughter move, he said, but would be free after seven. He also sent a list of restaurants, the last being a sports bar called Buffalo Wild Wings. I quickly chose that one because I didn't want to be in a quiet, dark, candlelit place with someone I didn't know and wasn't necessarily interested in. I knew if need be I could say I had to use the restroom then slip out of a crowded, lively restaurant unnoticed.

As Saturday drew closer, I began to regret agreeing to this meeting. When I expressed my reservations to my good friend, she replied, "You need to practice putting yourself out there and date. Besides, what else do you have to do?"

She was right about that; I had no social life. I assured her I would go and she promised to have her phone in hand in case I needed her help.

There were plenty of questions swirling through my mind as I drove the hour and fifteen minutes to meet him that night. We had never seen each other; we had never even heard each other's voices. What would he be like?

Clint walked in just ahead of me. I thought that was him anyway, so I called out his name. He turned around, smiled, and said, "Judy? I was just going to walk around and see if you were here." He then asked where I wanted to sit. I said at the bar would be great, so we grabbed two stools at the end and preceded to talk for three hours. Neither of us even got up to go to the restroom. We talked about our families, work, vacations, and lots of other things. It was really nice.

At the end of the evening, he walked me to my car and asked if he could see me again. I said I would like that, then he gave me a hug and we parted ways. I remember feeling really good and smiling a lot on the drive home. I was sure he wasn't the one, though, because he was nothing like I thought he would be. He wasn't my "type." In my mind, I was just putting myself out there, practicing dating.

The next day I went to my granddaughter's soccer game. It was a beautiful day and it felt great to sit in the sunshine and watch the kids play. Partway through the game I got a text from Clint asking if I wanted to meet for dinner. I immediately said yes and after the game I headed home to get ready. We met halfway this time, at a Mexican restaurant with outdoor seating, and after dinner took a walk on a trail close by. It felt so good to be with Clint walking down the tree-lined path, so good that when he reached out for my hand I didn't pull away. I did have a few concerns, though, and this seemed like the perfect time and place to ask about them. Clint was open and honest with his answers. He took responsibility for his part and I felt good about his explanations. Later, as I was about to slip into my car, Clint took my face in his hands, looked into my eyes, and kissed me more tenderly than I had ever been kissed. It was very different from what I was used to and at the same time felt so familiar.

Nine months later we were married. We have for sure had our bumps in the road and have worked through many challenges as we blended our families. Through it all, though, we have always known that love is the answer to any challenge. Looking through the eyes of love allows us to have grace for others as well as ourselves.

I know I could have easily missed my life with Clint had I not learned to follow my heart instead of my head. My head kept telling me he wasn't my type; in fact, I still sometimes look at him and laugh and shake my head in disbelief. I think he does the same with me, though he would never admit it. But he is absolutely what I need in my life. He has shown me what love is in so many ways. He shows me the strength in being vulnerable and sentimental. I always had these qualities, but I had hidden them under layers of being tough, strong, and independent. I thought I couldn't be both strong and vulnerable. What I know now is that being vulnerable is the greatest strength.

I learned to trust what I was feeling and it paid off. Clint and I don't have all the answers; we simply move through each day trusting that everything will work out and knowing we can handle it together. I am grateful to my heart for knowing what I need.

Be inspired:

My life changed when I paid attention to how I was feeling. That brought me the gift of being able to be vulnerable.

Journal Prompt:

Do you see vulnerability as a weakness or a strength? Why?

The Pause

"It is in the unwinding of our old story and rewriting it that we find the freedom to be our true selves."

Some seemingly small decisions have been the beginning of major changes in my life.

Sedona

In September of 2017 my friend Janice and I went to a four-day retreat nestled among the Red Rocks of Sedona. From the moment we arrived I fell in love with the place and its magical energy, and I knew the retreat was going to be transformational. The house was massive, with a huge entry that gave way to two wide hallways with several sets of glass doors. One hallway led to the bedrooms, each of which had its own bathroom. The other led out to a center courtyard, which was landscaped with lovely trees and flowering bushes. The house also had a large kitchen and open living room with a fireplace and a sunroom that led out to the pool and hot tub. There was a firepit and plenty of places to sit around it in the evenings. The whole place was bright and cheery and beautifully furnished. Oh, and did I mention we had the most amazing chef onsite to prepare delicious meals for us? I felt truly pampered.

I had "officially" kicked off my spiritual journey the year before at "Celebrate Your Life" in Phoenix. This was a three-day conference with spiritual teachers who taught classes on everything from card reading and past lives to mediumship and near-death experiences. Essentially, it's like a spiritual boot camp.

I learned about Celebrate Your Life while scrolling through Facebook one day in between clients. People whose books I'd read or who I had seen on Oprah would be teaching there. Sometimes you see an ad or hear about something and you think, *That would be fun* or *I would like to do that.* This was different; something inside me came alive and I just knew I had to go. I immediately called my husband and asked what he thought. He was so supportive, not only encouraging me to go, but offering to help me pay for it. A few weeks later, I was in Phoenix. At that conference I felt more in alignment with who I am than I had ever felt in my life. There, I found my tribe, I found a place in which I fit. It was a true awakening.

One of the teachers was Sunny Dawn Johnston. I hadn't planned on taking her class because I had never heard of her, but when I heard some ladies talking about what they'd experienced I became intrigued. The topic was vulnerability, and I remember walking into the space and thinking, "I'm already vulnerable, so maybe I won't have too much to learn." I thought it would be easy. Boy, was I wrong! It was the kind of class that either leaves you hungry for more or running away as fast as you can, screaming, "F#%! this, I'm out of here!" For me, it was the beginning of breakthroughs and extraordinary healing.

From the moment I met Sunny I felt an instant connection. I joined her community and started attending every class she offered online and in-person whenever I could manage it. It was hard work, and I'd be lying if I said I wasn't tempted to run a few times over the years, but I'm proud to say I've stayed with it.

At first, I didn't tell anyone, aside from my husband, that I was going to spiritual events. Friends and family assumed I was involved with continuing education for my work, which made sense as over my forty years as a hair stylist I had attended, worked, and facilitated hundreds of classes and events. While I loved what I did, I realized my spiritual growth had taken a back seat for far too long; now I was learning to grow in all areas of my life. I just wasn't yet ready to share it with others in my life.

Now, a year later, I arrived in Sedona excited and open, knowing I would experience whatever I was meant to. Sunny and Robin, her assistant and dear friend, greeted us at the door with hugs and lots of laughter then told us to leave our suitcases by the door so they could give us a quick tour. They also introduced us to several other participants – there would be twelve in all – who I had never met before. I was almost as excited about meeting twelve new "tribe members" as I was about the retreat itself.

After we got acquainted with our surroundings, Sunny and Robin said they would show us to our room so we could get settled in before dinner. We swung by the front door to grab our suitcases, then followed them down one long hallway and then another, past bedroom after bedroom. Just when I started to wonder if we would ever get there, we came to the end of a hallway that opened up into a small sunroom. Robin informed us that this would be where we would have yoga in the morning. In the corner of the room was a spiral staircase. Now, if you pack like I do, because you just never know what you might need, you're guaranteed to have a big suitcase. And if you've ever maneuvered a spiral staircase, you know it's not easy even without luggage. I inwardly groaned about this but I was determined to stay upbeat. We made it to the top of the staircase and there was a large bedroom with a beautiful screened-in porch and big windows everywhere with views of Cathedral Rock. The views were stunning! My eyes, however, were fixated on the furniture, specifically the one queen-sized bed, and the twin bed in the far corner. I felt a flicker of concern.

When I signed up for the retreat, I was told I would have a private bed and bath. The retreat was a big expense for me and I wanted to fully relax and get the most out of it. I also liked my privacy.

"Here's your bed!" Sunny said, smiling.

I smiled back, but I was thinking, *Then where's Janice's bed?* I looked at the single bed in the corner and figured it would just have to do.

"I will just sleep there."

Sunny laughed. "Oh, no, there's someone else in that bed."

WTF?

Then Sunny stepped forward and opened a door to show us our bathroom… only it was a half-bath, no shower. Now it was *really* WTF!

"Oh, and when you want to shower, just go to the bottom of the stairs to the right, through the laundry and mini-kitchen. It's a really nice big bathroom and some others may want to share it with you.

So not only do I have to share a bedroom and a bathroom, I have to drag my clothes and toiletries down this steep, narrow, staircase when I want to shower! I could feel the emotions start swirling, churning and wanting to come up. I had felt this many times before.

This, however, was the first time I remember pausing before I reacted to something I wasn't happy about. It felt so good not to have to regret what I said or did.

Now, don't get me wrong, if I had to pick someone for a roommate Janice would certainly be at the top of the list. I just like my space and was looking forward to having my own room. And, I had paid for it.

There have been many times in my life when things didn't go the way I thought they should, and oftentimes I reacted by getting pissed and making sure that everyone knew I had been wronged. In this moment, however, I recognized that I had a choice. I could do what I had always done and go straight into my victim story, or I could grow and expand into gratitude for having such a beautiful room with the best views and the best roomie. I am so happy to say that I chose gratitude. I chose to immerse myself in the beauty of the retreat and let go of the victim that had kept me from growing, and the result was magical.

That retreat left me forever changed. I met some of the most incredible people and made some lifelong friends. There were many lessons learned and old patterns interrupted. I was starting to get a taste of who I was under all the layers of unwanted emotions that I had never known how to handle. I was starting to experience freedom. The freedom to be me.

Be inspired:

Pausing can be instrumental in changing a pattern. When I felt the relief that comes from not having regrets, I wanted to change.

Journal prompt:

What pattern do you have that leaves you feeling regretful?

What are you willing to do to interrupt that pattern?

The Grace

"It isn't always clear in the moment, which moments will end up inspiring exponential growth for us."

Defining Moments

There are moments that define the rest of our life. Sometimes they are huge disruptors, other times they appear to be so small and insignificant that we barely notice them at the time. However, whether they stop us in our tracks or we remember them later, they can have the same effect on our lives.

For me, one of those defining moments was when I took my dad to the doctor and found out he had cancer. He was eighty-seven and had been slowing down a lot over the past few years, but otherwise he was in good health.

My dad was a really hard worker. When I was young, he had two jobs, one at a charcoal briquette factory. He would work the ten-p.m. to seven-a.m. shift, then come home, jump in the shower to wash the black dust from his body, and head out to the farm. In the summer he bailed hay for the cattle to eat in the winter, fixed fences, and cut wood, among other things. In the winter he chopped ice on the ponds and whatever else came up; this, in addition to feeding the animals and other daily chores. He would come in every day at six to eat supper then go to bed to grab a couple of hours of sleep before his night shift. The only time I remember him resting was on Sunday afternoons, when he'd lay on the couch watching the Cardinals play baseball and Chiefs play football. Sometimes he even took a nap. I remember how good it felt to see him relaxing for a while.

When my mom passed on in 2013, Dad was lost. He didn't know what to do without someone banging around the pots and pans in the kitchen and trying to tell him what to do. He was really sad and had some regrets, but he was so brave. Losing someone you've been with most of your life has to be terrifying. Plus, Mom's passing was a surprise. She was nine years younger than him, and had always been very active and young for her age. Everyone assumed he would be the one to go first, but it didn't happen that way.

After she passed, I started spending every Sunday night with my dad. I would cook, clean, and do his laundry for the week. It wasn't that Dad couldn't do those things, but I knew it brought him comfort, and it made me feel good to do it for him. In my whole life I had never spent so much time with Dad as I did on those Sunday evenings. We watched rerun after rerun of *Hee Haw* and he laughed like he had never seen it before. I remember him laughing like that when I was a kid about the same things on the same episodes! Sometimes we would sit for hours and not talk. I'm like my dad in that way; we didn't "talk just to hear our head rattle," as he would say. I treasured those Sundays.

My brother and I noticed that Dad was slowing down and not eating as much, but at first we weren't too concerned. When I cooked on Sundays he seemed to have a good appetite, so I thought maybe he was depressed and didn't like eating alone.

He had his regular six-month checkup and his longtime doctor told him he was fine. Knowing Dad, if he wasn't feeling good, he probably didn't mention it. He wasn't one to complain and if the doctor said he was fine who was he to say he wasn't? So when he told me and my brother that he needed to go back to the doctor, we took it seriously, especially when he didn't want to drive himself.

This time, Dad told the doctor he wasn't doing well. The doctor felt his stomach and said, "What's this? This wasn't here last week." Apparently, there was a huge knot in his stomach, and it had been there a week earlier; the doctor just hadn't examined him. The doctor ordered a CT scan later that morning, and we decided that I would stay while my brother headed back to work. They gave Dad some fluids to drink before the scan, then sent him out to the waiting room to sit with me until they were ready for him. Though he put on a brave face as usual, I knew he had to be feeling really bad; he had always hated going to the doctor and wouldn't be there otherwise.

Shortly after he finished drinking the prescribed solution he went into the restroom. I was immersed in a magazine article and when I finished, I realized Dad had been in there a long time. I waited a little longer, then knocked on the door and asked if he was okay. He said he wasn't. When I went in, I found my strong dad in a mess. I got him cleaned up as best I could and went to the store to get him some clean clothes. I was going through the motions, just doing what had to be done.

When the nurse came to take him for the test, she asked him how he was doing. He said, "This is the worst day of my life." As per usual back then, I stuffed down emotions and uttered a sarcastic remark to make light of his comment. How could having an accident, which he in no way could have prevented, cause the worst day of his life?

After the test results came back the doctor admitted him into the hospital and I called my brother to fill him in. When I told him about Dad's comment to the nurse, he seemed to understand what he meant. He found it degrading that he couldn't take care of himself and, he felt embarrassed and ashamed that his daughter had to see him like that. I, on the other hand, felt honored to witness the only time Dad had shown any vulnerability. Until then I don't think I even realized what vulnerability was. Growing up, we didn't dare admit we were struggling or needed help or understanding. That was a sign of weakness and only the strong survived. We stuffed every emotion down and the only acceptable release was anger. This was the first time my dad didn't show anger. Instead, he expressed how he was feeling.

Dad didn't get any better; in fact, his condition worsened quickly. He would not be coming home, nor could he stay in the hospital for more than a few days. We met with social workers and decided on a nursing home. We got all the papers signed. Dad would go there the next day.

After meeting with the social workers, my brothers and I grabbed lunch in the hospital cafeteria while my daughter and nieces kept Dad company. The cafeteria was like a nice restaurant with a buzz of activity. It was a good distraction. We went back up and were told that Dad was not doing well at all. I went in to talk to him, unable to believe that my strong dad looked so weak and pale. This was only the second time in my life I had seen him helpless. He had IVs and oxygen going. I could tell he was uncomfortable.

I looked at him and said, "Dad, it's okay if you go. We'll be fine. You can go whenever you're ready." I didn't plan to say those words, I wasn't even sure where they came from. He looked up at me and in typical Vernon fashion nodded his head and said, "Huh. Just give me a drink of water every once in a while." I smiled down at him through my tears and said, "Thank you for being a good dad, I love you."

"Thank you for being a good daughter," he replied, "I love you too."

Those were the last words I heard him say. A short time later my dad took his last breath, surrounded by his kids and grandkids.

My dad gave me the gift of experiencing the closeness that being vulnerable can bring. I am forever grateful for that, and I honor him by practicing it in my life. It's not easy, and sometimes I catch myself wanting to run. Then Dad pops into my mind and I remember what he showed me. It gives me the strength to feel and express my emotions.

We are souls in these bodies to have a human experience, part of which is feeling sadness and loss. After a lifetime of stuffing emotions down deep I am finding the value in feeling and releasing them. Being able to feel is what makes beautiful relationships. Sure, we don't like everything we have to go through, but every time we allow ourselves to feel and release an emotion it brings us closer to understanding who we are and what we bring to this earth. Our experiences, pleasant and unpleasant alike, bring blessings and expansion in the lives we live. It's all about how we choose to define those moments.

Be inspired:

Some of our defining moments seem insignificant when they happen. They lie quietly hidden in our subconscious mind just waiting for us to slow down so we can experience the magic they hold for us. The awakening happens in perfect Divine timing, when we are ready to receive and cherish their gift. Then we are forever changed.

Journal prompt:

Write about a defining moment in your life that revealed itself sometime later.

How did it reveal itself?

What did you learn about yourself?

What changes did you experience in your life?

_____
_____
_____
_____
_____
_____
_____
_____
_____
_____
_____
_____
_____
_____
_____
_____
_____
_____
_____
_____
_____
_____
_____
_____
_____
_____
_____
_____
_____

The Shift

I have learned that healing can come through unexpected people in miraculous ways.

One Friday night, Jason, my daughter's ex-husband and the father of her four kids, came for a visit. This was a surprise as the grandkids had thought he wasn't coming until Saturday morning. My grandson was particularly excited because it was his thirteenth birthday and he wanted his dad to spend the night.

Three of my grandkids had come to stay with us when their living situation with their mom became unstable. This was nothing new. The kids had lived in many situations that I didn't think were healthy. This time I feared for their safety and moved them out and in with us. I dropped my daughter off at a hospital for rehab.

Jason had had his share of struggles too and was not actively involved in the kids' lives. My daughter had full custody and did not think his situation was stable enough for the kids to spend time with him.

A few months earlier I would never have believed he would be welcome in my home. When he was married to my daughter, he was into lifestyle choices I didn't approve of. He was a very different person then, but so was I. I would love to say that our strained relationship was all his fault. He didn't keep a steady job, was drinking and doing drugs, and kept the grandkids from me if I didn't help them out.

It was easy to blame him.

At the time I was judgmental and unaccepting of anyone who didn't do what I thought they should do. Of course, I would never say anything, I didn't have to; it was easy to see by my demeanor.

I did love Jason's mom, Stella, though, and we stayed in touch after he and my daughter divorced. When Stella had a stroke and wasn't doing well, I would FaceTime time her every Sunday so she could see and talk to the grandkids. I took my granddaughter to see her and even cut her hair for her a few times. She was thrilled! We never talked about our kids and the problems they had. We only talked about the love we had for our grandkids.

Not long after that she passed away. My daughter asked me to take the kids to her funeral, and I agreed even though it would be awkward being there with their dad. I hadn't seen or spoken to Jason for years. He was in jail at the time and had to get a pass to attend the funeral.

As we headed to the funeral home, my thoughts were on my grandkids and the challenging day that lay ahead of them. Not only did they have to say goodbye to their grandmother, they had to deal with the anxiety of seeing their father for the first time after such a long absence. They were also worried about how Jason and I would get along as neither of us had ever hidden our dislike for each other.

Jason arrived a few minutes after we did. I'm sure he expected me to be the same to him that I'd always been. I'm sure he thought I would hover so he didn't do or say anything wrong in front of the kids. That's how I had been in the past. I expected him to have the same arrogant attitude he'd always had towards me. But when I saw him, something inside me changed, and we could both feel that shift.

When I saw him, a miracle happened.

It was unexpected and beautiful.

My love expanded in ways I couldn't have imagined.

There were things in my life that I felt frustration, anger, resentment, and other heavy emotions around. I had buried most of them, thinking they weren't important. I had moved past them. That's what I would tell myself.

I told myself that about Jason. He was in the past and an insignificant part of it. I didn't have to deal with him ever again. To be totally honest, I thought of him as being insignificant because of the way he lived his life.

I didn't see the opportunity for healing that was coming for me, and I certainly didn't think it would come through Jason.

When I saw him, I thought he looked like a lost, sad, fearful little boy. That was the first time I had ever seen him that way. I had always seen a monster when I looked at him. An angry, selfish monster.

Now, I felt as if Stella was guiding me from the other side; she was guiding me to help her son in a way that only I could on that emotion-filled day.

"He isn't what he's done. He isn't his shortcomings," she whispered to me. *He can heal, and you can heal...love heals everything.*

The kids ran to their dad and hugged him. Tears streamed down his face. He was dressed in black pants and a gray shirt. He looked good but I could tell he was uncomfortable.

He told me how grateful he was that I'd brought the kids.

I told him how sorry I was and how much I loved his mom. Then, to my great surprise and his, I asked him if I could give him a hug.

We hugged for a long time. All those things we had said to each other and about each other melted away in that hug, in an instant.

For the first time, we could see each other for who we really were. It was a miracle!

During the service I sat in the back of the chapel and the kids sat with him. It was a great comfort for him to have them there. After the graveside service we gathered for lunch. Jason shared a lot about his journey and the changes he was making in his life. I told him how proud of him I was, and how proud his mom was. I shared with him that I felt her presence and guidance that day. I felt she was helping us both change. He thanked me several more times for bringing the kids, and apologized for the things he had said and done in the past. I did the same.

I also encouraged him to stay strong with finding a new life. I told him I believed in him and would think of him often. The more we talked the lighter I felt. An incredible weight had been lifted from me. A weight I hadn't even known I was holding. That's when I realized that the healing wasn't just for Jason, but for me as well. For this reason, and though I was saddened by her passing, I will always look back on the day of Stella's funeral with gratitude and awe of the transformative power of love.

Love is a miracle. It changes anger and resentment to compassion and empathy in an instant.

Love happened when I got out of the way and took my power back from judgments I had made.

Healing is all around us; we just have to be open to it. Healing often comes in unforeseen situations and through the least likely people. We just have to be ready for it, as Jason and I were that day.

To do this, we must see ourselves in others. What I realized that day was despite our circumstances, we both had struggles – it's just that his were on the outside, there for all the world to see, while mine were hidden on the inside.

I couldn't love Jason while holding his actions against him. I had to see our likenesses instead of our differences. I had to see him for who he was, not what he did. I also had to love myself to forgive the things I wasn't proud of.

I am forever grateful to Jason and Stella for showing me my authentic self, which is love.

That weekend at my home after his release, Jason and I talked and laughed like old friends. He shared the changes he was making in his life and how he'd helped fellow inmates do the same. The kids loved having him, and I loved cooking for them all, especially since I knew Jason didn't get a lot of homecooked meals.

He also shared a lot about the dark times in his life and about how he grew up. There were a lot of things I hadn't known before, and hearing them gave me greater insight into him and some of the life choices he had made in the past.

How many times do we judge others for the choices they make and how they live?

As soon as we make a judgement, we block the flow of love. We look at our differences instead of seeing our sameness.

Be inspired:

Have you missed opportunities to heal because you thought the other person needed to change in order for you to change?

Journal prompt:

No matter how insignificant a struggle seems, I believe it holds a lesson for us. Write about a struggle you have experienced.

Ask yourself about your part in the struggle. Are you ready to let it go?

Expansion

When a great ship is in the harbor and moored, it is safe, there can be no doubt. But that is not what great ships are built for.

– Clarissa Pinkola Estes

The Vision

"Live for the moments you can't put into words."

Without a doubt, the best money I have spent in my life has been the money I've spent traveling. Travel has filled my heart, broadened my perspective, and left me with the gift of stories to share. Every trip inspires me to grow more into who I am.

Thailand

In November of 2018 I was part of a group that went to Thailand for two weeks. As we boarded the plane in Los Angeles, I was excited, but I had no idea what a life-changing trip it would be, or that I would meet twenty-three beautiful souls I now consider dear friends.

Up to that point, I had been to some cool places – Mexico, Grand Cayman, the Bahamas, Hawaii – but none as far away as Thailand. This would also be the first trip I had taken by myself where I didn't know everyone I was traveling with. In fact, other than the people organizing the trip I didn't know anyone, not even my roommate. This was a real leap of faith for me. When I saw the trip advertised, I knew immediately that I had to go, similar to when I saw the ad for the Celebrate Your Life conference. Have you ever had that experience? You see something and instantly felt a connection to it? It really doesn't make sense, you just feel a strong desire to go. For sure, Thailand was on my bucket list of places I wanted to experience. I'd just thought it would come later in my life, you know, when I was prepared for it. One thing I have learned is that there likely won't be a "perfect" time for the things you want to do in your life. You just have to go when the opportunity presents itself and trust that it will all work out. I have experienced magic when I do this.

I purposely didn't research a lot about Thailand before the trip. I didn't want any preconceived notions that would keep me from being open to what I saw there. I wanted the whole trip to be filled with wonder, and that meant experiencing Thailand in the moment and from my heart, not my head.

Our group met in Los Angeles to get acquainted before boarding the plane for the fourteen-hour flight to Beijing, China. After a five-hour layover there, we flew for six more hours to Bangkok, where we would spend our first few days. The city was alive with people, riding scooters, cooking in the streets and selling jewelry and trinkets. You could buy a full meal for about two U.S. dollars, though we were cautioned not to buy from street vendors. And it was all about families; they worked together, preparing food and making other items to sell. They clung to each other – mothers, fathers and children – as they rode their scooters through the crowded streets. What struck me most was the palpable sense of peace about the place. Despite the appearance of chaos, there was no yelling or cursing at each other to get out of the way; everyone seemed to be in a flow of patience and tranquility, in this city of some ten and a half million. My guess is that many of them only know that way of life. The Buddhist influence is also a contributing factor to the lifestyle and mentality there.

The second day in Bangkok was spent touring temples. Most of them were centuries old and kept up by donations from visitors. They were magnificent, with beautiful detail work everywhere. I most vividly recall the Temple of the Emerald Buddha. Our guide, Jym, told us that all Thai people travel to Bangkok to visit this temple for the new year. They pay homage to the Emerald Buddha, believing it will bring them great blessings. It is also the most popular tour for travelers from around the world.

Judging from the length of the lines to get in, it seemed like everyone had decided to visit on the same day. The crowds, coupled with the heat – typical for Bangkok in November, (it was in the upper nineties and humid) – and the fact that we had to cover our arms and legs before entering, made things a little uncomfortable.

58

This was when I truly began to appreciate being a part of a group tour. Jym, who seemed to know everyone who worked in all the places we went, quickly got us to the front of the line. As we approached the entrance, she directed us to take our shoes off and put them on a rack. I eyed the huge shoe racks – there must have been twenty of them – and wondered, how would we ever find our shoes again? Jym also warned us that there were a lot of pickpockets in the area and to keep our hands on our purses and keep them in front of us. That seemed odd to me, but there were signs everywhere with that warning.

From the entrance of the temple, I could see magnificent paintings on the ceiling. There were beautiful statues and carvings everywhere. The colors were brilliant and the craftsmanship was like nothing I had ever seen. Everywhere I looked there was a beautiful work of art to behold. We weren't allowed to take pictures, so I was taking pictures in my head in an attempt to remember all the glory I was seeing.

I walked into the temple behind Jym along with two others from our group. The instant we entered the temple, there was an undeniable feeling of reverence and peace. I had never been in a place that felt like that. It was hard to describe. I felt like I entered another world. As we walked closer to the front, I could see an area that was roped off. The sign said, "Thai people only." This roped off area contained the statue of the Emerald Buddha. It was on a beautiful pedestal that looked like it was made of gold. This sacred area was reserved for Thai people to worship.

Jym left us there and went back out to escort more of our group into the temple. As we stood gazing about in awe and amazement, the man who was guarding the roped off area looked at us, smiled and invited us in. I looked around, thinking he must be talking to someone behind me, but he smiled again and motioned for us to enter. There were only a few other people in the area and they were immersed in their worship.

It is hard for me to describe what happened in the next few moments; to say it forever changed me would be an understatement. I knelt down and, following the lead of the other worshippers, stretched out my arms and put my face to the floor. I felt tears starting to stream down my cheeks. I didn't feel them coming on and there was nothing I could do to stop them. I felt the presence of the Buddha, Jesus, Mother Mary, Mother Theresa, and every other ascended master. I felt a warmth and a love that I can't explain. It was the most unconditional love I have ever experienced. I didn't have to do anything, just my presence there was enough to deserve this great love. I can only describe the feeling as "I am home." I did not understand how this was possible; all I knew was that I felt its truth in the core of my being.

I'm not sure how long we stayed in that sacred space. It seemed like hours but I'm sure it was probably just a few minutes. We got up and walked outside to find our shoes and the rest of the group. All this time, a steady stream of tears flowed. There was nothing I could do to stop them. Maybe somewhere deep inside I thought my tears would keep me in that place where I felt such reverence and love. Maybe it was the only way I had to express emotions that I had never experienced before.

I found my shoes, got them on and finally got myself together. I knew this trip was going to be a time of exponential growth for me. I couldn't wait to have some time to process and journal my thoughts and feelings. Later that night I wrote, "My heart is full! If this is the only thing I get to experience in Thailand, it is enough." But there would be so much more…

Be inspired:

I believe that immersing ourselves in other cultures allows us to grow in empathy and compassion. When we learn about how people live and what their customs are and why, we gain an understanding of them.

Journal prompt:

What is your favorite place you have traveled to?

What did you love about being there?

What did you learn about yourself?

The Clues

"Our Mind is a beautiful servant, but a dangerous Master."

– Buddha

etting curious about memories that pop into our mind can lead to a deeper understanding of who we are.

At times, seemingly random memories will come into my awareness. Many of them are from childhood, and they usually come in the form of a thought. When I am busy or preoccupied, I dismiss the thought as being insignificant and go on about my task at hand. My mind says, "It was no big deal, why am I thinking about this?"

I'm not talking about remembering something that you know was life-changing. This is more about a nagging little memory that returns from time to time. As my awareness is expanding, I am learning to look at these with curiosity. I ask myself what wisdom have I've gained from this experience and why did this memory come to me at this time? I used to think I was the only person who had these odd experiences; now, of course, I know better. I believe that when we are present and get curious, we can unwind the magic and wisdom these memories hold.

Recently, I had an experience that taught me how looking deeper at these memories unlock a new understanding of self. Much of who we are comes from conditioning, and even more comes from what we tell ourselves about what happens to us. When we feel threatened, we make decisions that are from a fight or flight or a freeze reaction. Our mind takes us into protection mode as if our survival depends on it. We sometimes, without even knowing it, make decisions that create beliefs that live in our subconscious mind. Holding on to these beliefs significantly effects our lives. The problem is oftentimes these beliefs are limiting. They can keep us trapped in a cycle of being stuck. I have a very strong mind, a steel trap. I'm sure that has served me well... maybe... sometimes?

I learned from a young age to make decisions with confidence. Well, it looked that way on the outside anyway. I recognized that neither of my parents were good at making decisions, it seemed painful for them to decide on things, no matter how big or small. So I decided it wasn't a big deal; just make a decision and go with it. Now, there are two important parts to this. One is that when I made a decision there was NO turning back, NO admitting I was wrong, NO changing my mind. The decision was final. You might guess how that worked for me. Second is that I gained the awareness that I could not stand the uncomfortableness of not knowing. I felt too vulnerable with in-decision. At that time, vulnerability and indecision meant weakness to me. It was easier for me to deal with what came from the decision than to sit in the indecision. You probably don't have to wonder how this worked for me either, right?

During a morning meditation I had a memory from when I was six years old. I was at my best friend Dee Dee's house. I loved spending time with her, and I especially loved going to her house. It was almost like she was an only child. Her sisters were all teenagers, so they weren't around much. I loved it when they were there, though, because they were so beautiful and so cool. I didn't have sisters, so I loved watching them put on makeup and fix their hair. They had such beautiful clothes, all the latest fashions. I thought they must be very wealthy because their dad worked at the bank and I was sure he could just have all the money he wanted. Dee Dee had all the best toys too – the latest Barbie, Ken, and Skipper dolls, and a beautiful dollhouse that we would play with for hours. Being the youngest, she might have been a little spoiled. Her sisters got on her a lot when she was being bossy or not sharing. I imagine for her it was almost like having four moms. I could tell her sisters liked me, though of course I was on my very best behavior, especially when they were around.

That morning wasn't the first time this particular memory, this "picture," popped up. It had happened occasionally, and each time I had dismissed it as having no significance. And because I dismissed it, I never got past the picture. I never got quiet or curious enough to explore the possibilities it held for me. In order to do that, I had to "go back there" and observe. I had to unravel the feelings and let them lead me to the wisdom. For some reason, in that meditation, I did just that. I took myself back to that snapshot, the moment when Dee Dee and I were standing in her kitchen. We had taken a break from playing to get a snack. Her older sisters were sitting at the bar talking as their mom cooked dinner. I remember Dee Dee walking to the pantry, opening the door and demanding a snack. Her mom told her to wait because dinner was almost ready. Dee Dee got mad and started yelling at her mom, which was not unusual. Her sister said, "Why can't you be good like Judy? She doesn't act like that."

More beautiful words could never be said to a people-pleaser and, as mentioned, I was definitely one of those. I tried especially hard to get Dee Dee's sisters to like me. I loved getting attention from them. I was so proud! I felt my heart swelling and a smile brightening my face. This is what I lived for! I was soaking up this beautiful feeling of belonging and worthiness. That is, until I looked at Dee Dee. She was glaring at me with disapproval and anger. Then, in typical six-year-old fashion, she stuck her tongue out at me. As you can imagine, that only made things worse for her. Her sisters scolded her again. This was just kid stuff, right? Sure, unless you are highly sensitive, which I am.

In the past, I was caught up in thinking I had no right to feel the way I felt because many others had much more tragic things happen in their life. I have since learned that trauma can come from outer experiences and/or what we tell ourselves about those experiences. The decisions we make that live in our subconscious can do the same things that an outward tragic event can. There is no measuring stick for who gets to suffer the most. That's why these seemingly random memories pop into our mind. It is our Spirit guiding us to look at clues to what we have locked beneath the surface.

I went right back there, feeling all the feelings. I remember how excited I was to get to spend the night with my friend. I was excited to see her sisters and have them not only notice me, but give me the best compliment I could imagine. I remember feeling so good inside, until I looked at Dee Dee. Then I felt like I got too much attention and it wasn't safe. If my best friend was going to like me, I had to play it small and not get any attention. It may sound crazy, but I know the truth of it because I can *feel* it. I decided in that moment with my steel-trap mind that I could not stand out. People would not approve of me getting attention. I took this to heart and made an unconscious decision to not be seen. Later, the bigger events in my life just affirmed my decision. Remember, this was all unconscious. It kept me playing small and afraid of getting too much attention. It has held me back from sharing with the world what I came here to share. Until now.

Because I did that, I can now see the experience for what it was. I can see how that one little decision started to change who I was and how I showed up in the world. I see where that decision has weaved itself through many of my life's experiences. I can change that decision that I made so long ago. I do not need anyone's approval to shine.

Be inspired:

The memories that keep coming back to us hold clues to our wholeness. They contain the lessons that we came here to learn. Our subconscious mind holds them until we are ready to see the truth in them. We just have to get curious and ask what wisdom they hold.

Journal prompt:

Have you made a decision in the past that no longer serves who you are?

What decision can you make now that better serves the truth of who you are?

The Insights

"Life-changing insights come in a lot of different ways."

Horse Stories

*I*f we're open and receptive, we can experience miracles in very unexpected places. I gained some profound insights about myself thanks to a couple of horses named Dreamer and Cowboy.

I didn't grow up around horses and I haven't spent much time with them; I've ridden them only a handful of times. It's not that I disliked or was afraid of them – I actually thought they were quite majestic – I was just not drawn to them. It wasn't until I met my friend and soul sister Janice that I realized how intuitive and magical these creatures were.

Unlike me, Janice had had a lifelong connection with horses; in fact, they are an integral part of her healing work. Though I respected and was fascinated by what she did, I was harboring some skepticism.

"Seriously, what could a horse teach me?" I recall asking when she asked if I wanted to have an experience with them.

Janice flashed me her sweet, innocent, little-girl smile. "Oh, you'll see."

I trusted her and felt sure she knew what she was talking about. Besides, what did I have to lose?

It was a beautiful, sunny day. As we walked to the barn, I felt a little nervous, though I wasn't sure why. Janice walked with me into a pen with a large, beautiful stallion named Cowboy. After giving me some safety instructions – basically, that I was responsible for not getting stepped on – she told me to just enjoy. Sure, I was thinking, but what do I *do*?

I decided that maybe if I focused on the smell of the fresh cedar shavings and the horses that I could get into the experience. And just in case you didn't pick up on it before, I have a busy head; I'm always thinking. My head is always telling me what I "should" do, think, say or be. As I'm learning to feel my way, instead of thinking my way through life, I know to get quiet so I can hear the whispers of my heart.

When I tried to pet Cowboy, he walked away, and my best effort to stay in my heart began to fade. *He doesn't want YOU to pet him,* my mind said, *Don't chase after him.* That was how I perceived the situation. In reality, Cowboy was walking to the other side of the pen to take a dump. As soon as he finished, he returned to my side. I thought it was very considerate of him to walk away to do his business so I didn't have to worry about stepping in it.

"See," Janice said, "He wants to be by you."

My thought – "He came back because you're here" – must have come out of my mouth, because Janice turned around and left the pen. Cowboy stayed right by me.

Janice gave me a look and said, "What do you want?"

"I want to pet your damn horse!" I replied. The snarky tone was my way of dodging the feeling of being vulnerable.

Janice didn't respond, and in the awkward silence that followed I heard my heart say, *Go for what you want. Stop making excuses.* Wow! I was well aware of my history of making excuses about why I couldn't have or do something. However, I had been learning to stop blaming others and circumstances for unwanted things in my life. Now my victim mentality was once again rearing its ugly head, indicating I still needed some work. Cowboy was reminding me to focus on what I want.

"Okay, got it," I announced proudly, "No more excuses. I am done."

Janice wasn't convinced. "Oh, I think there's more. Cowboy is still right by you."

I turned to the horse and for the first time noticed his intense focus on me. As I looked into his eyes, his bottom lip began to quiver. Tears filled my eyes. In the silence, my heart spoke. *It is safe for you to feel your emotions.* That was a message I really needed to hear. I had spent my life stuffing my emotions so I didn't have to feel pain. Problem is, I could only feel love and connection to the degree I allowed myself to feel the pain. I was learning that in order to live life fully I had to be vulnerable and open, no more stuffing down and not feeling. I am still not sure how a horse can see things and teach you things about yourself that you don't know or don't want to know. But I can tell you I have experienced it in profound ways.

I am forever grateful to Janice and Cowboy for ever so gently guiding me to heal aspects of myself I didn't even know needed healing so I could live my best life.

Be inspired:

I spent much of my life caught up in limitations instead of focusing on possibilities. Being open to experience things I don't understand has provided me expansion in all areas of my life.

Journal prompt:

Think about a time that you struggled with a perspective different than your own. What if the struggle was there because your heart knew another perspective? Write about what comes up for you. Are you willing to open yourself up to different possibilities?

Dreamer

When I arrived at the Shift the Script event I immediately knew Dreamer would be a challenge. He is a beautiful horse, and very spunky. He had extra locks on his gate because he had figured out how to slide the latch and escape. I had also watched as Dreamer pushed my friend Lynn around and gave her a run for her money. So instead, I picked Holly for my first encounter. She was sweet, calm, loving and, unlike Dreamer, seemed to be an easy guide. I thought easy was a good place to start.

I had traveled to Arizona from Missouri for the event. It was so great to be in the warm sunshine for a few days and connect with some very special soul sisters. I was looking forward to expanding in self-awareness while having a break from my normal routine and from the cold. Being surrounded by the desert and all its beauty would be good for my soul.

As I was petting Holly, she closed her eyes and rested her head in my hands. I felt such connection. I was fully in my heart. I heard, *Connection is always available; it's inside. I can feel connected any time; all I have to do is have that awareness.* Holly's message was comforting and aligned with what I know.

When I left Holly's pen, I could see Lynn still handling Dreamer. She was laughing and amused with his shenanigans, and for some reason I found myself drawn to spend time with him. I squeezed through the fence so I didn't have to go to the trouble of unlocking multiple locks on his gate. I thought the playful horse would be fun, but it didn't take long for me to become annoyed with him nipping at me.

I stopped petting Dreamer and walked outside. He followed me. I thought since he followed me that must mean he liked me. As a recovering people-pleaser, I like being liked, so I continued to overlook Dreamer's behavior. He kept pushing and nipping, and finally I told him to stop in a firm voice. After several more warnings, when he still didn't stop, I climbed back through the fence.

You might think I was annoyed with Dreamer, and that's true, but I was annoyed with myself too. You see, what I realized is that I have never been good at setting or holding my boundaries. This has to be about boundaries! I got quiet for a moment and heard my heart whisper, *You can't expect someone to change because of your boundary. The boundary is not about their behavior; it's about what you will or won't allow. It's for you, not them.*

A flood of memories flashed through my mind of expectations I had around people honoring my boundaries. I can't tell you how many times in my life I have changed or dropped altogether boundaries I had set. I gave others countless opportunities to "change." Just so you know, neither worked very well for me.

In the short time we spent together, Dreamer showed me the flawed way in which I had viewed boundaries. They were not there to change other people; they were there to demonstrate that I honored and valued myself. This was an epiphany so profound I knew it would change forever the boundaries I set, and therefore my relationships with others and with the world.

Be inspired:

Be open to new ways of finding out about your hidden aspects. Horses are highly intuitive creatures and naturally guide you to your "blind spots" so you can see with a new perspective.

Journal prompt:

How do you get insights into yourself?

What profound things have you learned about yourself in an unexpected way?

The Truth

*"Everything you were looking for was
right there with you all along."*

– The Wizard of Oz

When I was young, the Wizard of Oz was shown on tv once a year. Every time I watched was special, but I will always remember the time I figured out that the characters Dorothy met in Oz were actually the people in her life. So many lessons and so much magic in that movie – this is why to this day it is one of my favorites.

Throughout my life I've spent a great deal of time thinking that other people had something special that I didn't have. I told myself I was not born with their special, even though when I said that, I would hear a quiet voice say, *Everyone has it.* I stood by and watched as others seemed to effortlessly express who they were, what they wanted and to go after it. I admired their confidence and certainty. On the other hand, I was sure I couldn't have what I wanted. Many times I found myself settling for what was "easy"; that was good enough. I told myself I was lucky to get what I got; I heard that a lot growing up. Even though I didn't think it was fair that others could have or do things that I couldn't, I didn't question it. To want more meant that I wasn't grateful for what I had. I didn't question that either.

In my mind, settling for easy was better than falling short of what I wanted. If I fell short of what I wanted, I would be disappointed and would have to admit failure or defeat, which was definitely not an option. That's how I saw things at the time – win or lose. I did not have the curiosity to ask if there was another option. It was not easy for me to see possibilities. My beliefs were fixed and rigid yet there was a part of me that knew there was more.

For as long as I can remember, I've had within me a soft whisper that kept reminding me that I had something special too. I had a hard time believing that, so I didn't listen. I found evidence everywhere that I was right. I spent my time proving to myself that I wasn't worthy to have what others that I admired had. I built layer after layer of excuses for not showing up for myself.

Some of you might think that the more layers and the further away from the whisper I was, the easier it got to ignore it. I'm here to tell you that's not the case. Instead, the gentle whispers grew louder, and the ache in my heart grew stronger. I think this happens around midlife when we ignore our inner knowing. Maybe that's where the "crisis" part comes in. It wakes us up to make sure we give proper attention to ourselves and our quiet longings. It lets us know that time is moving on and we've ignored our essence long enough.

My Spirit was done messing around. It was time to get moving. Half of my life was lived and I was still ignoring something important to me that I came here to do. Sure, I'd filled my life with good things and had some happy moments. By many standards, I was doing great.

Yet the world I had created on the outside didn't align with what was in my inner world. I longed for real connection and that started with myself. If I was going to have an authentic life, I first had to admit to myself what I was hiding behind. As mentioned, one of the behaviors keeping me stuck was avoiding painful things. I was a master at that. I didn't want to feel pain. It was uncomfortable and from a young age I did everything I could to keep from acknowledging it to myself and anyone else. It wasn't until I began my spiritual journey that I became aware of the many times I had stuffed down the pain of disappointment or sadness. Problem is, that only lasts for so long. Eventually the pain has to come out of the body. I could store it up for days, months or even years, then in an instant I would offload it onto some poor, innocent bystander – usually a family member – who was just in the wrong place at the wrong time. Have you ever gone crazy over spilled milk? I sure have. I would blame them for my outburst, then feel guilty and critical of myself. I was so busy caught up in this cycle of self-defeating behavior that I didn't have time or energy to experience or create the life I dreamed of.

It might sound silly, but I didn't even know what it was that I wanted. I just knew there was a longing in my inner world that, despite my best efforts, would not be silenced. How would I discover what others had that I didn't? What were they doing that I wasn't? I had no trouble expressing what I *didn't* want in my life. I knew I was exhausted and ready for change. I always want to know what I need to do right now; cut to the chase, give me the quick-read version so I can get this over with. Anyone else like that?

In case you don't know, it doesn't happen this way. It took years to pile on the layers of limiting beliefs, so we're not likely to unravel them in the blink of an eye. This, by the way, is actually a good thing. Whether we boldly go for our dreams or we stumble upon what we're looking for, it will take time for them to unfold. It is our life's work to discover and express what lies buried deep inside us. We all come here with unique gifts and talents; we all have something special. No matter what we do, we all have something to experience and share with ourselves and with the world.

I believe that we begin to grow and expand when we get curious about the possibilities that exist outside of the ones we know. I started asking myself what it was that I admired the most in the people I thought had it all together, had direction in their life, and were happy most of the time. I started observing how they acted and reading their books. It didn't take long to figure out what these people had in common.

The people I admire the most in my life know that within them exists a purpose greater than themselves that longs to be expressed and shared with the world. Their special isn't about what they do, it's about *how* they do what they do. These people don't let what others say, do, or think affect the way they show up. They know who they are. They know that unexpressed gifts cause pain. They have fears and have learned to power through them in order to be who they are. They stand for what they believe and are not afraid to express it. They don't need approval. They are authentically who they are, without apology.

I am unraveling my "special" more every day. I am doing what my soul has been longing for me to do all my life. It's really pretty simple. Just get quiet and let the inner nudges and whispers lead the way. Ignore the "mean girl" voice that holds you back from being your truest self.

Be inspired:

"You've always had the power, my dear,
you just had to learn it for yourself."

– The Wizard of Oz

Journal prompt:

What is your something special?

Is it buried under layers of "not enough"; "not worthy"; "only other people get to have and do that"?

What is it that you need to express? Get quiet and ask. Be present and feel it in your body.

The Adventure

"The world is big and I want to have a good look at it before it gets dark."

– John Muir

The excursion I had looked the most forward to on my Thailand trip was the day with the elephants. I didn't know what to expect, but I was all in! It was hard to imagine being face-to-face with such majestic creatures.

On the morning of our fifth day, we boarded the plane for our short flight from Bangkok to Chang Mai. I had taken a lot of pictures in Bangkok; this was the trip of a lifetime for me and I wanted to remember every detail. So far, everything was going on schedule and smoothly, and I was excited to explore more of this incredible country.

In Chang Mai we got to stay at a property that held retreats for monks; in fact, we were the first group of tourists allowed to stay there (our tour guide, Tina, had pulled some strings to make that happen). It was a beautiful, serene place. The grounds were spacious with bright pink flowers and trees all around. The area had a jungle feel to it. There was lush green vegetation covering the landscape. Some of the group had beautiful individual huts with stone walkways connecting them. Some of us stayed in the main building. The unit we stayed in had a spacious living room, dining area, kitchen, two bedrooms and two bathrooms. It was perfect! It also had a covered deck with comfy lounge chairs and a view of a lake and beautiful trees. It was a perfect, relaxing change from the hustle of Bangkok.

The first day we spent time exploring the property. As we strolled along the trails, we learned about some of the plants and flowers native to the area. We spent the rest of the day at our leisure, then met for dinner.

The restaurant had a large outdoor seating area on a stone patio that had a spectacular view of the sunset. I tried some Thai dishes I had never had before and found them to be delicious. I also found my favorite Thai beer, Chang. Then it was off to take a nice long bath and go to bed.

I always get up early in the morning, usually around five. There was a twelve-hour time difference from home, but I had no trouble adjusting to the difference. I attribute that to being in the present moment, and I had never been more in the present than I was on that trip. I didn't think about what time it was at home, just what time it was there. Those early hours on the covered deck were amazing. It rained softly each morning and there was fog rising off the lake. You could hear monkeys and birds in the trees and monks chanting in the distance.

We boarded the bus for the short drive to Baanchang Elephant Park, a refuge for elephants that had been rescued – some from circuses, some from farms. Others had been abandoned because they were getting old. The care that the elephants got at Baanchang was amazing. Each elephant had its own handler who was pretty much by its side twenty-four/seven. It was a small family-owned operation and they had been taking care of elephants there for more than thirty years; their knowledge had been passed down for generations. It was evident that these creatures were sacred to them.

The first thing we had to do was change into some, well, let's just say not-so-stylish clothes. They were bright royal blue, capri-length, wide-leg pants with a drawstring waist and the same color shirt. This lovely ensemble was completed with a straw hat that had matching royal blue trim around the brim. We were quite a sight!

After we dressed, we had lunch, which was absolutely amazing. We started with Tom Yum Soup, a favorite Thai soup filled with vegetables and shrimp. Next was crab rangoon, followed by Chicken Pad Thai. And for dessert, a wonderful assortment of fresh, locally-grown fruit. While we were eating, our guide filled us in about what to expect on the tour. He told us about how the elephants were cared for, what they ate, how much they ate, and many more interesting facts. Eventually we walked to the area where the baby elephants stayed. There were three babies at the time and each was in their own pen. Their handlers watched over them like overprotective mothers, and were vigilant in making sure that everyone followed the rules and treated them with the respect they deserved. The babies loved the attention of their handlers and visitors alike, especially when they petted and scratched them behind their ears and fed them sugar cane. Being sprayed with water from a nearby hose was another favorite, and they played and seemed to be having as much fun as we were.

After spending a while with the babies, we were given bags filled with bunches of small, ripe bananas to take to the elephants in the field. This was where the elephants got to graze and roam for most of the day. Before we were allowed to go into the area, our guide introduced us to each of the magnificent creatures and their handlers. We were told their ages, their history, and how they came to Baanchang. Some of the stories were sad. Some of the elephants had been chained up their whole lives, others had been in the circus, and others had been beaten while working on farms. I was so happy that they had a good home and were well taken care of now.

Our guide then went over the rules of how to approach the elephants, including how to hold out the bananas for them to take. Finally, it was time to experience these beautiful creatures up close and personal. The elephants were free to roam in the grassy field with their handler by their side. They seemed so peaceful and happy. I stood in the middle of that green, grassy field, arms outstretched, the sun warming my skin, and knew I was living my dream.

"I am in the middle of a field, in Thailand, with elephants... in the middle of a field, with elephants, in Thailand." I repeated this out loud several times, soaking it all in. I'm pretty sure I added, "Holy Shit!" a few times as well. I will always remember how I felt in that moment. It was magical and surreal, for sure, and I felt blessed beyond measure.

With that, I started to wander around the field.

Though I no longer recall her name, I remember being particularly drawn to the elephant that was rescued from the circus. She seemed to wander off from the others; she seemed like a loner. I walked toward her, full of excitement and anticipation. Wait, shouldn't I be afraid of being in a field with these enormous creatures freely roaming about? What if they got scared and started running? It's not like the handlers could stop them from trampling me! I quickly shut those thoughts off, deciding that nothing was going to ruin this experience that had been gifted to me.

As I neared the extraordinary creature, I felt a peace and calmness come over me. I reached into my bag and pulled out a bunch of bananas. That got her attention. She turned her head toward me and reached out with her trunk to retrieve her treat. I held them flat in my palms, just like instructed, and she grabbed them and with one fluid motion, deposited the entire bunch into her mouth. I just stood in amazement at what I was experiencing. I moved around to the front of her and got out another bunch of bananas. This time, I reached past her trunk and put them directly in her open mouth.

In Buddhism, the elephant is seen as an earthly manifestation of the qualities embodied in the Buddha himself. They epitomize his endless powers of wisdom, patience, loyalty, and strength. As I looked into the eyes of this incredible creature who had endured such suffering, I knew in my core that this is true. I felt the wisdom she held in her gaze. I felt her eagerness to share what she knew. I stared into her eyes for what seemed like hours, and I felt her telling me that anything was possible and that I have great strength within me that will appear when I call upon it. Tears filled my eyes, and my heart was full of gratitude. I rested my forehead between her eyes and thanked her for her message. I let her pick the bunch of bananas she wanted out of my bag. Our guide told us they like to do that. With that, I went on to meet the rest of the elephants.

After our time in the field, we were led by our guide, the handlers and the elephants down a dusty path to a small lake. The elephants knew where we were going and seemed to be excited. As we got to the water, they entered, one by one. The handlers went in with them and motioned them to lay down. The water was only about waist deep, so the elephants weren't completely submerged. Our guide came around with scrub brushes and plastic bowls. He had the handlers show us how to scrub the elephants while we poured water on them.

Now, I was not at all sure that I should get into this very dirty water that elephants had likely pooped and peed in. Some of the group decided not to. I stood there for a minute, wrestling with myself. *You will get some kind of disease from that water. I can't believe that you would actually get in. What if you get really sick and have to go to the hospital and miss the rest of your trip?* As all this mental chatter was going on, I saw people starting to go into the water and scrub the elephants. I was hearing their laughter and seeing the joy on their faces. My thoughts then became: *I did not come all the way to Thailand to stand by and watch others bathe these elephants. This trip is about being all in and experiencing everything I can.* I took my brush and bowl and went into the murky water to tend to my new friends. It brought me joy to see the elephants relish the water and the scrubbing. They seemed so content. I was glad for the "stylish" outfit I had been given, which saved my clothes from having to be thrown in the trash. You'll be glad to hear that I showered right after bathing the elephants and did not contract any diseases from the dirty water.

I believe that being immersed in other cultures gives me insights into parts of me that I didn't know about. Being open to new and different experiences changed my perspective and my life. I can't wait for Peru in 2022!

Be inspired:

If it's not a little scary, you're not stretching yourself. I am always all-in when I travel. I want to experience it all!

Journal prompt:

If you could go anywhere, where would you go? Why? What do you want to experience there?

THE ADVENTURE

Connection

God dwells within me. As me.

– Elizabeth Gilbert

The Words

Recognizing and celebrating that we are all inextricably connected to each other by a power greater than all of us, and that our connection to that power and to one another is grounded in love and belonging.

– Brené Brown

I believe we all have words, thoughts, ideas, and wisdom to share with others. I like to think of them as gifts. These gifts can come in the form of a thought you share during a conversation. They can come in a text, a phone call, or a greeting card. When we are guided to share these gifts and learn to act on this guidance, we have the potential to uplift and transform, not only the receiver, but ourselves as well.

Potential

I've always felt I have the gift of being able to see things in others that they can't see in themselves. Regardless of a person's external circumstances, no matter what they have done in the past, I can see a myriad of possibilities for them. What I didn't realize is that sometimes others don't care about their possibilities. They are good with the way things are. Oh, and there was one other small detail I overlooked: it wasn't up to me to decide what someone else should do to feel fulfilled. Yep, the control freak likes to surface, especially when I can clearly see how perfect things could be for someone.

Before I had clarity around this gift, I often got caught up in the possibilities. In other words, I was living in what I saw as possible instead of the current reality of what *was*. I also assumed that because I thought those possibilities were great, someone else would too. Does that make sense to anyone? I spent years of my life thinking that everyone knew what I knew and felt like I felt. I had to do a lot of unwinding to get out of the fixed mindset I had.

I remember a conversation I had with a coworker about her potential. At the time, I had been working with Allie for a little while, but she had already been doing hair for several years. What I loved about her was her curiosity and drive to learn more. She always wanted to know the *why*. I'll admit I sometimes wanted to say, "Because I said so," just as I did with my kids. I don't think I ever did, though. At the time, Allie was in a relationship that wasn't going well and had some other things going on in her life. Things started slipping at work as well. I noticed she wasn't putting in as much effort as she once had.

It's hard to know when to share your observations with others. I think sometimes we wait for them to ask and other times we say what we're guided to say. I remember sitting at the nail station getting my nails done before work and Allie came and sat down. She seemed a little irritated. We made some small talk about the polish colors, then I made eye contact with her and said, "You have so much potential, Allie!" She looked me with a blank expression and then looked away. "You are unbelievably talented and so smart," I continued, "The possibilities are endless for you, girl!" She looked up at me again and I could tell she had no idea what I was talking about. All she could see at that time was what was going wrong in her life. It's hard to see possibilities when we are going through stressful times.

Still, I knew that was not the end of the conversation. I could tell that what I said had touched Allie's soul. She wasn't ready to receive it then, but I felt sure that eventually she would remember it. It was like planting a seed. I could see what was possible for her and knew she could have it. It was what I call a "God moment."

Not long after that, I went to work at a different salon but I kept up with Allie through social media and mutual friends. She was making changes in her life that were moving her in the direction of her greatness. With diligence and hard work, she became a master at her craft.

She became an artistic educator for a major hair brand.

Years later, I was out shopping and ran into Allie. We hugged and I told her how proud of her I was and how happy I was for her and all those she was helping. She said she remembered our conversation when I told her how much potential I saw in her. She said at the time she had no idea what I was talking about, but she kept playing it over and over in her mind. As she stayed true to herself, she found those gifts. She was able to recognize the strengths she had and build a life that she was proud of.

I'm happy to report that Allie's transformation has been nothing short of a miracle. She has overcome many obstacles with courage and bravery to be where she is in her life today! She openly talks about her journey and is an inspiration to many who are going through similar struggles.

Have you ever been speaking with someone and suddenly had a thought come to mind that you weren't sure you should share? Or, what about that thought, "out of the blue," that you should text or call someone? I sure have, lots of times. Oftentimes I stopped myself from sharing the thought or reaching out because of the reaction I thought that person would have. I thought it would sound weird or not make any sense to them. I didn't trust my guidance.

I believe we are all here to support and help each other. That support can come in lots of ways. I have thought so many times, *What if I hadn't shared those words with Allie?* I am certain she would still be where she is today, yet I like to think that she felt supported and valued because I shared. I got to experience the joy of seeing Allie thrive; that was the gift for me.

It is said that Spirit sends us hundreds of messages every day. How many of those do you pay attention to? As we become open to and aware of these guiding messages, our life becomes magical. Our magic is meant to be shared with others. We are not meant to do this alone.

I assure you that Spirit did not drop us here to fend for ourselves. We have been trained to look for our guidance outside ourselves and question what we feel and know inside, when it's actually the other way around.

Be inspired:

Life becomes full of possibilities when we follow our intuition and guidance, both for ourselves and for the others we touch.

Journal prompt:

Think about a time a thought popped into your mind to do or say something.

I find that those seemingly random thoughts are how my guidance comes. It took me a while to recognize them and follow through. I am grateful that I have learned to trust, even when it makes no sense and I do not get validation.

Trust that the memory or nudge that comes holds a clue for you.

Did you follow through with the thought, or did you dismiss it?

How will having this awareness change the way you recognize your guidance?

The Becoming

"All that we are is the result of what we have thought."

– Buddha

I would add to this, *"What we tell ourselves is not always true."*

My Little Girl

I have a six-year-old girl living inside me. She's perfectly content to stay unseen and unheard, safe in the background… most of the time. She's sweet, intuitive, sensitive, caring … and she's been hurt. The hurt came from well-meaning adults, friends, society, and life's struggles. I think the real pain, though, came from what she told herself – her critical self-talk.

This little girl learned to bury deep any emotions that would give away her true essence. She traded them for acting strong and indestructible. She learned not to trust anyone, especially herself. She pretended not to care so she wouldn't be hurt. This little girl made a decision to go it alone. It was easier than explaining how she felt. It was easier than feeling what she felt. So she stuffed all those emotions, all the pain, and even the joy, down deep. She took great pride in being so strong that she didn't cry. Showing emotions meant you were weak.

My little girl was most definitely not weak, she could handle ANY-THING. The more she stuffed down, the tougher she became. That toughness turned into a wall around her protecting her from judgement, criticism, and pain. It felt safe there, where she couldn't be seen. What she didn't know is that it was also keeping her from experiencing the love, joy, and connection that she so desperately longed for.

I was never taught how to handle emotions. I wasn't shown that it was safe to feel and express them. I believe that is true of many people. I'm sure my parents and grandparents weren't taught about emotions either. They were in survival mode. Survival for them was all about the physical world. Working to provide food, shelter and clothing. That's the only aspect of self-care that was important. It had to be addressed first. There was no time for emotional or mental care; it was all about survival.

I only recently came to realize that this little girl was still alive and fearful. She needed to be set free. She needed to have a voice. She needed to know she mattered. She needed that from the only person who could give it to her: the fifty-nine-year-old me. I was beginning to understand her like no one else could. She needed the vulnerable, trusting, loving person I've become to set her free.

Emotions can only be stuffed for so long before they erupt, believe me, I have experienced this. They come out sideways if you don't take care of them in a healthy way. I found out that when I felt triggered by what someone had said, it was actually my little girl being triggered. That's when I would make a snarky comment or walk away instead of asking the person what they meant. I took everything personally. This was all subconscious behavior from the limited perspective I had at the time. I had made my mind up years earlier that I was not enough and I thought everyone else agreed with me. When I compared myself or my life to others, I would come up short. That feeling would take me straight back to a powerless little girl who only knew how to express anger – the only emotion that was allowed and understood when she was growing up. I expressed anger when I felt sad, confused, scared, or any other emotion I didn't know how to deal with. You only know what you know until you learn something else.

I have learned a lot about emotions from Clint. I know, usually it's the woman who knows about matters of the heart, and in a way that's the case here as well. You see, Clint had the best teacher: his mom, Norma.

She was a loving, kind, caring woman who saw and brought out the best in everyone she knew. Clint and Norma were kindred souls; they would talk for hours about everything and nothing at all. Some of Clint's fondest memories are of Sundays, after family dinner, when his mom washed the dishes and he dried them. They would laugh and have a great time. Their bond is the foundation of who Clint is. He was so blessed to grow up in an environment where it was safe to feel and express emotions. I didn't even know such a space existed growing up! I always thought everyone was like I was – and thank goodness that's not true!

Clint and I have learned a lot about each other since we got married, and we've come to appreciate our differences. He is really easygoing; I, on the other hand, not so much (though I'm more easygoing than I used to be). It also took me a while to get used to Clint expressing his emotions. It's not that he was overly emotional, mind you, I just thought it was unnecessary for anyone, especially a man, to show that they were sad or disappointed about something. My own stuffed emotions usually came out in the form of "suck it up," and in fact I would sometimes catch myself thinking this when he told me how he felt. As I've mentioned before, I didn't think he was my type, and my kids definitely couldn't imagine me with him! I still laugh sometimes because they're right; however, he has shown me many, many times over how wonderful life can be when you're true to your feelings. He shows me that being open to loving deeply is safe.

It also took Clint a while to understand that when I made a sarcastic comment, it was because I was hurting. When you hurt, you lash out so others can feel your pain. You project your pain onto others so you can offload it and feel better. Problem is, that relief lasts only a split second, then you see the pain you inflicted on the other person. Whenever I saw the pain in Clint's eyes, I would deeply regret whatever I had said to him. Sometimes that regret turned into shame and I wanted to retreat back into hiding, safe behind the wall that protected me from my feelings. I'm proud to say that with time and a lot of work,

I have learned to reconnect with that beautiful little girl and find the courage to stay present and feel.

Clint is a great teacher; and he's been very patient. He says it's worth it. I didn't get to meet Norma – she passed on before we met – but I think about her often and am forever grateful to her for raising such an amazing son.

The awareness that I now have helps me to understand how to feel my emotions. When I feel them, I don't stuff them down or hide them in a nasty comment or look. I let them move through me and embody the gifts they bring. I know I am deserving of these gifts and the richness they bring to my life. Allowing myself to feel my emotions has changed my life. I am no longer closed off from the possibilities I imagined as a child. The love, trust, connection, and joy I longed for were right where I left them, buried deep inside. I am honored to create this life and I am forever grateful to that little girl within me for never giving up on her dreams.

Be inspired:

There isn't anyone who understands your inner child the way you do. This means that you can give yourself what others didn't give you. As an adult you can give love and understanding to a part of you that needs it. Oftentimes, we don't realize these parts just want to feel accepted. When we accept all our triggered parts, we can free our inner child. That freedom allows us to live with an open heart.

Journaling Prompt:

Close your eyes and picture yourself as a child. Answer the following questions in a story about that child.

How do you feel when you see this child?

Is your child happy?

Is your child loved?

Is your child well cared for?

Visualize you holding yourself as a child.

What does your child want you to know?

Ask what you can do now, as an adult, to comfort them.

The Message

"We don't always understand, and we don't need to."

Knowings

*H*ave there been things in your life that you were called to do, even though you had no idea why? Maybe it started with a random idea popping up in your head that just kept hovering there. The thought seems random and you can make no sense of it, so you dismiss it. I've had many random thoughts that I didn't act on, and after a while they went away. Then there were ideas that started out as gentle nudges and became louder and more persistent until I had no choice but to acknowledge them.

One such idea came to me on the way to work early one morning. We owned two businesses at the time, and I had to make a stop by our store before going into the salon. As I rounded a curve in the road, I could see the sun coming up over the horizon. The beautiful yellow and orange colors of the sunrise filtered through the trees.

In that moment of stillness and peace, I heard a voice say, *You need to speak at your grandma's funeral.* I thought that was really odd, for a couple of reasons. First, I was in the car alone and, second, my Grandma Agnes wasn't dead. Sure, she was in her nineties and living in a nearby care facility, but as far as everyone knew she was doing okay. I usually visited her a few times a day, and when the weather was warm and sunny my kids and I would take her out to the courtyard and have picnics. She loved to watch the kids play.

I don't recall what my thoughts were in that moment; I only remember the uncontrollable tears flooding down my face. I vividly remember this because I am not one who cries a lot. Plus, at that time I was pretty much in control of everything in my life (or so I thought). I was especially in control of my emotions back then. I stuffed them down so far they had no chance of emerging.

I got to work and went about my busy day, but I could not stop thinking about my experience in the car. I did not share it with anyone. I was unsure what to think about it. Finally, I decided that if I ignored it, it would go away. I was right about that. Weeks and months went by without my giving it another thought.

Eventually, Grandma Agnes's health declined and she passed on. Her last days were a celebration, with her loved ones gathered around her. She had a large family – nine children, seven living at the time. Their lives had not always been easy, to put it mildly. I didn't know much about those times because no one ever talked about them, but I could always feel that there was a lot of unresolved sadness for all of them.

My mom and my aunts and uncles got busy making funeral preparations. Relatives flew in from out of town, several decisions had to be made, and there was just a lot going on. It was busy for me too because I had family staying at my house.

Thoughts that I needed to speak at the funeral returned, but I hesitated to say anything because I really didn't want to do it. (Does anyone really want to speak at a funeral?) I did not mind speaking in front of a group; I for sure got nervous, but I could do it. A funeral would be different; I had never done that. What would I say? Could I do it without getting emotional? So many thoughts played in my mind. I decided I wouldn't do it. Besides, I was sure they'd already assigned everyone their parts.

Problem is, this time the thought would not leave. That "soft nudge," message, or whatever it was, grew more and more persistent until I finally approached my uncle, who was staying at my house, and told him I felt a strong desire to speak at the funeral. He said he thought that would be a great idea and asked if I had written anything. He offered to help me with it by organizing and typing it. Even though I had been telling myself that I wouldn't speak, I had been jotting down memories that I would share if I was going to speak. I handed him the papers with an apology and the hope he could make sense of it.

A short time later he came into the kitchen where I was cooking and handed me a neatly typed paper. I will never forget the look on his face when he handed it to me and said, "It's perfect, just how you wrote it." I read it and was amazed. It really *was* perfect! Wow! How had those words I scribbled down come together so beautifully? I was feeling good about my decision. I was thankful that I had followed the message, rather than letting my hesitancy turn into a regret.

Over the years I had learned the hard way about regrets. I knew how even the small regrets made me feel. Though they were things I might have another chance to do, I had a hard time getting over the fact that I'd let an opportunity slip by. I was learning that it was better to plow through my fear in the moment than allow it to keep me from something I wanted or needed to do.

By the day of the funeral, I was actually eager to share my memories. When it was time for me to deliver my message, I walked up to the front of the church, closed my eyes, and silently asked Grandma Agnes to be with me and take any nervousness away. As I began to speak, I felt a warm presence around me that was comforting and familiar. I felt so myself and alive. It was a beautiful tribute to a woman I was close to. I had no regrets about how I showed up in her life and no regrets about how I showed up after she was gone.

Some time passed, and as I was thinking about my grandma one day, I had an awareness. I realized she had needed me to speak about the good memories of her. I had experienced the very best of my grandma – I saw a side of her not everyone got to see. She had come here to do what she did in the only way she knew how, and now she needed to leave this life with good memories shared about her. I am forever grateful for that and for listening to the whispers that guide me to become more of who I am.

Be inspired:

Not knowing all the *hows* and *whys* requires us to trust that we will be led to the clues and people that will show us what we need to know. Our connection to Guidance is always there, we just have to be present.

Journal Prompt:

What are you putting off doing because you don't feel like you have enough information? Or because you think the time is not right, or because someone else might think it is stupid. Get the idea?

Trust

My life changed when I stopped trying to fit into a world that I didn't fit into and embraced my unique gifts. My life changed even more when I started to share those gifts and shine unapologetically. Then, others' lives changed.

The Return

"Our loved ones in Spirit are always near us, waiting for us to notice the signs they're sending us."

– Message from Grandma Agnes

The day after my grandma's funeral we had to go to the care facility where she had been living to move her things out. The manager of the facility needed us to clear the room as quickly as possible because they had someone else waiting to move in.

Grandma Agnes didn't have a lot of stuff. She had been downsizing for several years, going from a two-bedroom apartment to a two-room suite in an assisted living facility and, finally, to a nursing home when she wasn't able to care for herself. She had a small private room, just big enough for her bed, dresser, a rose-colored, velvet wingback chair, and a tv.

In addition to the regular visits from me and my kids, Grandma was fortunate to have a steady flow of others coming to see her. She loved seeing friends and family; it gave her something to look forward to.

My cousin described her best when he said, "She ain't no ordinary grandma." I think he made that remark at her ninetieth birthday party, where she was showing the grandkids how to dance the Charleston. Mind you, she had a walker, the kind with a seat, but she still had some moves! She had her two-year-old great-granddaughter climb on the seat while she danced, and they put on quite a show. I had countless other memories of her younger days as well. She was known for her love of playing Skip Bo and One, Two, Three O'Leary. I remember her playing jacks and jumping rope with all the grandkids. She loved Pepsi and Double Mint Gum. She loved to make people laugh.

That morning, I picked up some boxes to pack Grandma's belongings, then headed to the nursing home to meet my aunt and two of my cousins. I was assigned to clean the room out while other family members took care of other things that had to be done. I got that job because I find it easy to throw things away; I don't really get sentimental about stuff. My grandma was the opposite, so I was thankful that we got rid of most of her "treasures" before she moved the last time.

I got to the room and started packing and was soon joined by the others. We shared lots of memories and had lots of laughs. It was really nice to have family to help. It seemed like everything we picked up had a story. Several of the nurses stopped by to tell us how much they would miss Grandma. They all had stories to share about her too.

In the meantime, we continued to work, separating stuff going to the dumpster from the stuff to be donated. At one point the door slammed, but as we had the windows open and a nice breeze was coming in we didn't think much of it. Then my cousin Ryan picked up one of the boxes, intending to take it out to the dumpster, but when he tried the door handle, it was locked. My aunt and I weren't paying too much attention; we were busy going through dresser drawers. My cousin struggled with the door handle and couldn't get it unlocked. We all went over and tried to get the door unlocked. It was not budging. My cousin talked about jumping out the window and going around to unlock the door but he was afraid he would get stuck. The windows did not open very wide. We finally decided to use the call button and call the nurse's station to have someone let us out.

It seemed like it took an hour for a nurse to answer the call, though in reality it was probably just a few minutes. She tried the door and couldn't get it open from the outside. She told us she would have to find someone from maintenance to do it.

Before long a man showed up. By this time, we had everything packed up and ready to go to its final destination. Most of it was being thrown away since it wasn't anything anyone else would want. It was only my grandma who treasured those things.

After working on the door handle for several minutes without success, he knocked on the glass and said he had to go get more tools. Eventually he did get the door open, and then he looked up, shook his head and said, "Good one, Mary Agnes!" We all started laughing. "The doors in this facility," he explained, "do not have locks on them. It is not possible for the door to lock. For some reason Mary Agnes wanted to keep you in her room. She was a trickster like that!"

We all looked at each other and nodded in agreement; a shenanigan like that would definitely be something that Grandma would do.

Later, as I thought about getting locked in Grandma's room, I figured she didn't want us to leave. She liked us being together reminiscing about good times. Maybe she was trying to tell us to stay close. I wasn't sure what her message was.

That night I had a dream about her. It was a happy dream. She was surrounded by loved ones, talking and laughing. She was showing them all her most prized possessions. When I woke up, my first thought was that it wasn't that she wanted us to stay in her room. I realized that she locked us in because she didn't want us to throw her "treasures" away. She wanted us to keep all the birthday, Christmas, "Get Well," "Thinking of You," and any other cards she had. She treasured the pictures drawn by grandkids and great-grandkids. She kept them all. She loved all the little trinkets everyone brought her when they came to visit. She wouldn't let us throw any of that away when we would come and clean her room. She couldn't part with it and didn't want us to either!

Be inspired:

Look for signs from your loved ones in Spirit and you will see them.

Journal prompt:

Have you ever wondered if someone in Spirit is trying to communicate with you?

Death does not have to mean goodbye forever. We have deep connections to those we love that remains even after someone has transitioned. How could being open to experiencing your loved ones in Spirit bring you comfort?

The Magic

"Life is full of magical connections. We just have to know where to look." (Sometimes we also need a little extra reassurance.)

*L*ike most moms I know, I have worried about my kids from time to time. As hard as I tried not to worry and tell myself that they would be fine, occasionally doubt still crept in. I have a heart connection to my kids and can feel when they are struggling. I believe that heart connection is how we sense our loved ones might be in danger.

When they're little we worry about things, but we have much more control over what happens in their life. As they get older, we lose that control. I remember staying awake until they got home at night, breathing a sigh of relief when I saw car lights in the driveway. I would tell myself that soon they would be off to college, living on their own and I wouldn't know where they were or what they were doing.

I'd be lying if I said it wasn't a relief when the last of them flew the coop. There is a big age gap between my first two kids and the younger two, so I'd had kids in my house for thirty-six years! It was nice not to have to keep tabs on them constantly. Maybe it was because I was getting older and wiser that I didn't worry as much. Maybe I was just getting worn out! Maybe I was just learning to trust that everything would be alright. Maybe it's all of those. Then again, I'm not sure the "mom radar" ever fades away. My kids are grown and I still feel them when they're struggling.

I remember a few years back sensing this about David, my son. He was in college and living in an apartment on his own for the first time. I told him about my concerns and he dismissed them. I didn't push him, knowing I had to let go, but for some reason this seemed harder to do with him. Maybe it was because he was my youngest or maybe it was because he was my only son. All I knew is that the thoughts wouldn't leave. I had to do something.

I thought prayer was a good option. Well, a better option than hiring someone to follow David around and keep him safe – and not to mention cheaper too! I knew Archangel Michael was the angel of protection so I would call on him to watch over my son.

I don't pray in the traditional way I was taught to pray as a child. My prayers are usually more like conversations. Sometimes they even contain some negotiation on my part. I'm not sure if this is good or bad, but it seems to work most of the time. I sat down in quiet meditation to ask Archangel Michael to watch over my son. I said something like this:

"Archangel Michael, I have a feeling that my son could use some protection. I'm not sure what's going on, but I am concerned about him. I need you to watch over him closely, don't let him out of your sight. I want you to go everywhere with him…everywhere. I don't want anything to happen to him. It would be a little weird if I moved in with him, not that he would let me. It's not in my budget to have him followed. So, you are my only hope here. Please help me and watch over him. Oh, and I believe that you heard me, and I trust that you can do what I asked. I really do. But there's one more thing: I need to know for sure, without a doubt, that you are with him. I trust you, but I have to know so I can stop worrying. Let me know in a way that can't be overlooked. Thanks!"

Okay, so maybe not everyone would really consider that a prayer. I just put it out there, hoping for help. I decided that I needed to trust that my prayer would be answered, so every time worry crept in, I would say "Archangel Michael, take care of him." Weeks went by and I felt a little better. I was still looking for proof that he was being protected, though.

One day David called with some exciting news. "Mom! I'm getting a dog! He is a really sweet dog!" David was talking fast, not letting me get a word in. I'm sure he didn't want me to tell him it was a bad idea. We already had two dogs, and I knew David would be home for summer break, which meant now we would have three. "He's about four years old. He's been trained good. He really needs a home, the people that have him can't keep him. I really love him."

Just when I was thinking about all the extra fur on the furniture, he said, "Don't worry, Mom, he's a really good dog. He's super friendly, he's so cute. He's brown and has short hair so he doesn't shed bad." He paused long enough for me to ask him what kind of dog it was. He said "He's a pit bull, but don't worry, Mom, he's super gentle. Pits just have a bad reputation, they're not all aggressive, it depends on their owner and how they were raised and how they're treated. I promise he's not mean. You know that in other countries pit bulls were used to watch over and protect kids when they were playing outside. They are known as the 'Nanny Dog.'"

"Nanny dogs, huh?" I said, "So what's his name?"

"Mike, his name is Mike."

You just can't make this stuff up. I'd asked Archangel Michael to not only protect my son but to let me know for sure that he got the message. I didn't know what that confirmation would be, but I could have never guessed it would come in the way of a "nanny dog" named Mike.

I know for sure that he is protected. That doesn't mean that things won't happen, it just means he's not alone and neither am I. I trust that everything happens for our highest good. Sometimes we don't see that in the moment. Knowing all is for my highest good gets me through the tough times. There is help all around us. We just have to ask.

Be inspired:

We have support and assistance for everything we need, all we have to do is ask, believe, and receive.

Journal prompts:

Do you ask for signs from Spirit, your guides, or the angels?

Journal about signs that you have experienced from Spirit. Did you immediately recognize that it was a sign? Did that sign have special significance for you?

The Signs

*"Our loved ones in Spirit are always near
to guide and comfort us."*

– Guidance from Norma

*A*s mentioned, I didn't get the honor of meeting Clint's mom in person, but I do feel like I've gotten to know her through stories shared by her family. Mostly, I've experienced her by experiencing the love she showered her sons with.

Anyone who knew Norma loved her. She was a rare person. She had a way of making everyone feel special. She did this in her every thought, word, and action. It came naturally, it was her true essence. She didn't require or even want recognition; it simply was who she was. The memories shared about Norma are all filled with love. When her name is mentioned a sweet, soft smile follows. I imagine that's how Norma smiled.

There are times that Clint really misses his mom and gets sad. He used to talk to her every day in person or on the phone. She was a great comfort to him when he needed support. I, of course, feel his sadness; I feel his sense of loss, yet at the same time I feel like she's here with us. I can sense her presence close by, especially when Clint is sad. I can feel her love for her son all around, giving him comfort.

This is sometimes hard for Clint to hear, and I get that. It is true that it's not the same after our loved ones leave their physical form. We miss seeing them and hugging them. We miss experiencing them in the ways we were used to. But that doesn't mean we can't communicate with them; we just have to open ourselves up to different channels of communication. We have to quiet our minds and be still in order to see, sense, feel, hear and smell the signs our loved ones send us.

Norma's birthday has always been particularly sad for Clint, and this year I really wanted to do something to make him feel better. I just wasn't sure what that would be.

It was a beautiful, sunny Sunday, and we had been visiting my family; it's about a three-hour drive, round trip. Clint was especially quiet, and I knew he was thinking about and missing his mom. On the drive home I started to think about what to fix for dinner. Then an idea popped into my head. I can ask Norma what I could fix Clint that he would enjoy. I wanted it to be something that would remind him of times with his mom. He always talked about what a good cook she was. I wanted there to be no doubt that she told me what to cook. Okay, and I think I said it had to be quick and easy. Almost before I got the thought out of my head, I heard, *Manwich*. What? Are you kidding me? Manwich? Do they even make that anymore?

I'm not sure what I was expecting, but I know for sure it wasn't Manwich. For those of you who don't know, Manwich comes in a can and you put it on hamburger to make sloppy joes. I didn't recall ever fixing it, and I was sure I was getting in my head. I was doubting my abilities to connect.

"Okay, Norma," I said, "if they have Manwich at the small market by our neighborhood I will buy it, fix it for Clint, and tell him how you guided me."

Now, even as I made this deal with Norma, I was one hundred percent sure the store wouldn't have it. They had only a small grocery section with a very limited selection and they couldn't possibly have something so unpopular as Manwich.

I made up my mind that I would ask if I didn't find it just to be sure. I went into the market and halfway down the food aisle, right next to the tomato sauce, was... Manwich! I couldn't believe it! How could this be? Was I the only one who didn't appreciate this tasty treat? Whatever the case was, I felt like I'd hit the lottery! I grabbed two cans and headed for the register.

When I got home, Clint was in the garage. I asked him if he was hungry. He said he was and asked what we were having. I said, "How about sloppy joes with Manwich?' He gave me a strange look and said, "I haven't had that since I was a kid, I love it!' At that very moment I swear I heard angels singing and saw light streaming down from the heavens, just like in a movie. You *really* can't make this stuff up!

I went into the kitchen, thrilled to be making a childhood favorite dinner for my husband – not to mention one that was quick, easy, and pretty much foolproof. We sat down to eat and Clint shared that his mom used to fix Manwich every Sunday night for dinner. They would sit down at 5:30 to eat and watch the Wonderful World of Disney.

He then asked why I'd thought about fixing Manwich since I had never made it before. I told him the whole story – how I'd asked his mom for some help. How I'd wanted him to have something that reminded him of his childhood and her cooking. How Norma had let me know that Manwich would do just that. He looked a little apprehensive and said, "No, really, why. Are you sure I didn't tell you that?" I shook my head and told him about the "deal" I had made with his mother, that it had to be in that particular store. Then, at that very moment, we looked up at the clock and saw it was 5:30 on a Sunday evening!

I know for sure it wasn't the same as having Norma there in physical form, but we got to experience her love and caring from the other side. We both got to feel her warm compassion and caring nature as we ate dinner, on the same day and time that Clint had as a child.

Our loved ones in Spirit are available to guide and nurture us any time we ask. We just have to be open to receive messages from them in the way they send them, instead of the way we expect them to be. We must think about them being present instead of being gone. Their Spirit is around us waiting for us to notice and reach out so they can communicate with and support us.

Any time I want to comfort Clint I ask his mom for guidance. She is always right there, excited to share perspectives from a higher place. She is in a place of love and belonging. She sees the human struggle we have and lends her wisdom. We have so much help and guidance all around us. We are never alone, in joy or in struggle.

Be inspired:

We can find comfort in knowing that our loved ones in Spirit are still near us. We just have to be willing to experience them in a different way.

Journal prompt:

Journal about how it would feel to know that your loved one in Spirit is always available to help and guide you.

Surrender

If you suddenly feel very light, clear, and deeply at peace, that is an unmistakable sign that you have truly surrendered.

– Eckhart Tolle

The Wonder

"Love doesn't always feel like Love."

When I think back on my life there are two distinct parts: before my quest for spirituality began, and after. We all experience things that inspire us to look at ourselves in a different way. Sometimes it starts with a slow unraveling of beliefs and thoughts we have held about how things are or how they "should" be. As I worked through these pieces through journaling and meditation, more would be revealed to me. That was how most of my awakening occurred, step by step with gentle guidance. Then, there is the other way it comes, which I call "being broken open." I have learned to appreciate both ways of awakening, although the unraveling can certainly be the easier of the two.

Being broken open will occur in all our lives. It comes with death, divorce, and major loss of any kind. These are times that change us forever. Oftentimes we initially don't realize that we have choices in how we come out of these situations. We have the opportunity to grow and expand, or we can fall into feeling sorry for ourselves and blaming others for our feelings. It's been really easy for me to fall into victimhood. For a long time, I didn't realize that I was in charge of my happiness or that it came from inside and wasn't based on external circumstances. Of course, we grieve over the losses we experience, but we know we do not have to become bitter and resentful.

Other times, it's not something tragic that leads to a breakthrough of this magnitude. For example, I know it's possible to experience being broken open when the truth of who we think we are is challenged. This happened to me very unexpectedly a few years ago. Come to think of it, it only makes sense that we don't know these things are coming. If we did, we would armor up with excuses and all kinds of protection that would not allow the wisdom they bring to touch our heart.

When I was in the beginning stages of learning about myself (my spiritual journey), I thought I was much further down the road of understanding than I truly was. I mean, come on, I had watched Oprah and read the books her guests had written. Wasn't that enough? I thought I didn't have that much to learn, that I had it mostly figured out. I guess I *did* have a lot figured out from the very small world I was living in. I had closed myself off to the vast possibilities of my life with my fixed, rigid mindset. I was living from my ego; I didn't know it was possible to live from my heart. My head, with its constant negative chatter, drowned out my longing for connection and love.

A few months after I first met Sunny, I signed up for a three-day class I saw advertised on her website. It was being held in Phoenix that January, and I thought how perfect it would be to head to the desert, away from the snow and cold. Everything was working out perfectly, as the day after the event ended, I was to meet friends in Las Vegas for a hair show. It was a short, inexpensive flight from Phoenix to Vegas and I was excited to join them for some fun.

The class was a Mind, Body, Spirit Practitioner Certification Course. I wasn't sure what that meant but I was very drawn to take it. The course description sounded so interesting – we would be learning about how the mind keeps you stuck in unwanted patterns; how what you feel in your body is an indicator of your Guidance; and a lot about Spirit, including mediumship. There would be ten people in the class, most from the Phoenix area, and I didn't know any of them.

I remember feeling so out of place yet so in my element at the same time. I was really nervous but I was sure I was hiding it well. The first day, Sunny said, "Oh my! We have some very 'heady' people in our group." I wasn't exactly sure what that meant but I was sure she was *not* talking about me. Being heady, it turns out, means you have a very busy mind and a lot of mental chatter that takes over your experience. That was me for sure! In fact, it was such a part of who I was that I didn't even recognize it.

The first day went really well. My head was spinning from everything I had experienced. I was so grateful that one of my classmates offered to drop me off at my hotel. I couldn't wait to get there and be alone to sort through all the new ideas and information from the day. I got some dinner from the hotel restaurant and headed to bed early. I was exhausted and yet I felt so alive. I couldn't wait for the next day.

The second day we were going to talk about mediumship and have an experience around it. I knew very little about that. I had some experiences with my Grandma Agnes after she passed but that was about the extent of it. And those experiences had just happened, I didn't have to call them in. As far as I knew that's how it worked. Sunny taught us about how the Spirit world communicates with us and what we could do to strengthen that practice. Then she announced that it was time for some practice.

I could feel the excitement (or was it nervousness) in the pit of my stomach. I was also feeling a little apprehensive, thinking this would not work for me. *Great, what if I'm the only one who doesn't have an experience? What if everyone else already knows how to do this? Okay, I can fake it and make up a story. But what will I say? I can't make the story too big or they will know I'm making it up. I hope I don't have to go first...."* Get the idea? My head definitely kicked in.

I was relieved to be paired with Janice (who, by the way, is the same Janice who introduced me to horses and has become a dear friend). She was quiet, kind, and so sweet, and I instantly felt like I could trust her. We were instructed to sit facing each other with our knees touching and holding hands. I had done a few of these exercises in another class I took with Sunny, and they definitely tested my comfort zone. Who am I kidding? One part of me was excited for the connection and the other part of me was telling me to run like hell. But I had traveled a long way and spent a lot of money, so I was not going to let fear hold me back. I was all-in!

We closed our eyes and Sunny guided us to think of someone in Spirit who we wanted to connect with. My mind went blank; I couldn't decide who to choose. As Kris, Sunny's Soul Musician, played a beautiful, calming song in the background I relaxed a little. Sunny said to imagine the person standing behind us with their hands on our shoulders. This was the moment, mentioned in the beginning of the book, when I connected with my mom in spirit. I just *knew* she was there. I could feel her hands on my shoulders and a warm comforting glow that I had never felt from her before. Wow! Was this real or was I dreaming? The warmth of the tears streaming down my face affirmed that it was indeed real. I could feel that it was, in every cell of my body. I'm not sure how much time passed, but it seemed like a lifetime. Then I heard my mom's voice say, "I did it FOR you."

From my earliest memory my relationship with my mom was strained. It wasn't apparent from the outside, but I felt it on the inside. We got along, she was a good mom to me and I was a good daughter to her. But her tumultuous childhood had caused her to be manipulative. She didn't get the love she needed as a child. Her parents didn't have it to give to her. It was a generational pattern. I always felt like I was under her control and trying to please her. I had spent my whole life trying to love her enough so she could or would love herself. I had devoted my life to that when I was very young. She had done the same with her mom.

"I did it FOR you." Those words rang in my ears. I felt like I was going to break wide open. I couldn't breathe or focus. I felt like I knew nothing about my life. *How could this be? What do you mean? I thought I was the one teaching you to love yourself. I was taking on your emotions and trying to make you happy. Because if I could make you happy, that would mean I was a good girl and did my job. Then I could be happy.*

When the exercise was over, we were asked to share our experience. I was still barely able to speak. I felt lost. I cried as I described my mom's presence and what she had shared with me. "I should have known. I should have been able to see that. How different would both of our lives have been if I had known this while she was here? I can't believe I didn't know."

In her comforting wisdom, Sunny softly responded, "What if you weren't supposed to know, what if this is how it was supposed to be?"

Situations in our life can be so much different than we think they are. It's all about perception. Learning that everything happens for me and not to me has changed my life. I didn't realize that I was living deep in a victim mentality. My mom didn't verbally ask me to do any of what I had done. She probably didn't even know I was doing it. My mom had done the same with her mom and so had my grandma.

My mom was my first and one of my greatest teachers. She was an amazing person. She had so many beautiful qualities that I admire. She was teaching me to love myself. She was teaching me that I am responsible for my own happiness. She was teaching me to put myself first. She taught me all these things by not doing them for herself. These were all things that had frustrated me about her.

I've come to realize that when I feel frustration or am triggered in any way that there is something in myself that I need to look at. The other person is a mirror for me to see myself. This has not come easy for me, however, the freedom that comes from knowing I'm in charge of how I show up is life-changing.

Be inspired:

Be open to learning through new experiences!

Journal prompt:

How do you experience your loved ones in Spirit?

Do you sense their presence?

Do you smell their favorite perfume or cologne?

Do you hear them talking to you?

Do you have a knowing that they are with you?

The Guidance

"My life flows with grace and ease when I trust my Guidance."

I remember sitting at work one morning not long after I started questioning everything in my life. The sun was streaming in through the window and felt so warm on my face. I have always loved the feel of the sun shining on me. I feel protected when I'm surrounded by its warm light.

I looked up and asked, "What is it? What is missing in my life?"

At that time in my life, it wasn't often that I got quiet enough to listen or pay attention to thoughts that popped into my mind. But for some reason, as I sat in the warm sunshine that day, I did.

Like many of us, I had filled every moment of my life with busyness – family, work, kids' activities, friends – anything so I didn't have to think. I would be so exhausted at night that I fell asleep as soon as my head hit the pillow.

As I sat there, my Grandma Zimmer suddenly came to my mind. That was odd because I really wasn't close to her. I didn't even know her very well, and I never spent time alone with her as a child. There were always adults around and they were always busy talking; kids were to be seen and not heard.

Puzzled, I kept wondering why I thought about her. I knew she'd worked hard, and had a tough life on the farm. It was all about survival in those days, preparing all summer to have food in the winter. I thought of how hard it must have been to have six kids to provide for.

Yet, looking at Grandma Zimmer, you never would have known things were tough. She never complained, and she had such a sweet smile.

That was it! She was peaceful. As hard as her life was, she had peace.

Could it be that what I was looking for was peace?

I certainly wasn't finding peace in how I was living. I was in the rat race of working to acquire the next thing I wanted. And it made me happy until the newness wore off and I wanted something else. Going on a vacation always made me happy, until I got home and found things exactly as I had left them.

How could Grandma Zimmer have peace when she had so little and worked so hard? Could it be that peace comes not from our outside world, but from inside? With that thought, the sun seemed to feel even warmer and I knew that was my answer.

Okay, that sure sounded good, but how did I find peace? I didn't know, however, I thought that if my grandma could have peace in her life then I could surely find peace in mine.

We've all heard the saying, "Be careful what you ask for." Well, I'm here to tell you it's the honest-to-God truth, my quest for peace looked anything but peaceful.

When we ask for something, we expect it to be delivered within two days, as if we ordered it from Amazon. We even expect it to be in a beautifully wrapped package with a lovely red bow. Nice and neat! I thought peace would just come to my doorstep and become a part of me. You know, without much effort on my part. You see, I thought for sure that the Universe would swoop in and change everyone and everything in my life-change them so I could have peace. Sounds good, right?

The Universe works a little differently from that. When we ask for peace, it brings to our attention everything that is not peaceful so we can look at it and make the changes necessary to create and become what we desire. For me, this meant the "perfect" world I had so carefully and willfully manipulated began to crumble around me. Would I choose peace, or would I stay and keep fighting the things I couldn't change? I decided that despite the challenges in my life, I would find peace.

Guidance can come in a myriad of ways. A random thought can pop into our head, we get curious and keep following the clues. Before long, we have clarity and direction. People and situations show up at the very moment we need them to.

That's how we are meant to live our lives. There are possibilities that we can't imagine, yet from a higher perspective, they are clear. We just have to trust.

My Grandma Zimmer will always be a special part of my journey, not because I knew her well or spent a lot of time with her, but because she showed me her authentic self. She showed me that our inner world can be whatever we choose, no matter what's happening in our outer world.

The story of my Grandma Zimmer's influence goes even further.

Years ago, before I started writing, I asked my dad if I could have a table he had in the dining room. It used to be in the smokehouse, back when my Grandma and Grandpa Zimmer lived on the farm, and it was covered with dirt and lard drippings. My mom was going to throw the table away until her brother offered to restore it. It came out beautifully and I had always loved it. Now, thinking it would make a great desk, I put the table in an alcove in my bedroom in front of a large window.

Later, as I sat down to pen my first words, Grandma Zimmer came to mind. I knew it was no coincidence that I was sitting at her table. My grandma had inspired me to find peace within myself and it had led me to share that peace with others through my writing.

Be inspired:

The Guidance we receive may not always make sense at first, but if we are curious and get still long enough, the answers will come to us.

Journal prompt:

What magic have you experienced from following your Guidance?

Do you have resistance to accepting your Guidance? How can you overcome it?

_____
_____
_____
_____
_____
_____
_____
_____
_____
_____
_____
_____
_____
_____
_____
_____
_____
_____
_____
_____
_____
_____
_____
_____
_____
_____

The Unexpected

"Blessings sometimes come when you least expect them and in ways that you couldn't have imagined".

Blessings During a Pandemic

Over the past few years I've been slowly coming "out of hiding," meaning I'm remembering who I am. It started by going to those spiritual events, then taking some classes to learn more (and, as mentioned, telling people I was going to hair shows so I didn't have to explain or justify to them what I was doing). With each class and event my interest grew stronger and I longed for more. I was remembering so many things about myself. I say "remembering" because everything I was learning about myself was so familiar. It was like coming home. I had found my people!

I jumped in fully last year when I joined a mastermind group. In this gathering of ten beautiful, amazing soul sisters we discuss anything and everything; nothing is off limits. We are challenged to become the greatest version of ourselves that we can imagine. Our fearless leader guides us through the joys and obstacles we face with her intuitive teachings and love. Being part of this group has changed my life in ways I didn't know were possible.

One of my goals from the beginning was to get a website and build a social media presence. I didn't know why I was going to do this, but I knew it was in my heart. By the end of 2019, I had created a Facebook group and was posting regularly. I also had pictures taken for a website and social media content. I loved them and excitedly contacted a few people to build a website, but nothing seemed to work out. I started to think maybe I wasn't really supposed to have a website – I mean, what was it for anyway? Time went on and I got busy doing other things, putting the thoughts of a website out of my mind. Looking back, I can see the timing just wasn't right. The Universe was lining up the desires of my heart to be delivered at the perfect time.

I've learned that when something is put in my heart it is there for my growth and expansion. What is in my heart holds blessings for me. I've learned not to force things or try to make them happen. This has been a big lesson for me because for most of my life I've been a make-it-happen-any-way-I-can-this-minute kinda girl. (Is there anyone else like that out there? Tell me I'm not alone here.) In the past when I decided I wanted something I would not let go until I got it. Maybe that's why my dreams weren't any bigger than I could make happen on my own. I was depending only on what I knew or saw right in front of me. The problem with that is we see from the limited perspective of the human mind. We can't see all the possibilities that are truly available. Don't get me wrong, I did make things happen and got what I wanted, sort of. By this I mean I was in the habit of settling for less than I *really* wanted. I constantly told myself it was good enough. I was so impatient that I was willing to settle rather than wait for things to align. That led to feelings of disappointment and defeat. It left me feeling like I didn't deserve anything more than what I got.

I'm learning to wait for inspired action to be revealed. I don't get it right every time, but I'm definitely getting better. The Universe lines things up in perfect divine time in ways we can't imagine. All we have to do is be present and open to receive so we don't miss it. I wonder how many things I've missed because I was so preoccupied trying to make something happen. I wonder how many times I made things harder than they needed to be because I was forcing and manipulating the outcome.

We've all heard the stories of millions of people who had to transition to working from home when the pandemic hit. There were also millions more for whom this wasn't possible, and as a hairdresser, I was one of them. There was no work from home for me. The salon I work in closed for six weeks, the longest stretch of time I had been off since I started working at fifteen. I wasn't sure how I felt about this. I was used to being busy. I thought maybe this would be a great time to finish painting the trim and deep clean the house. I made my list of to-dos the first day off and got started.

Within the next few days, I saw an ad on Instagram offering one-on-one coaching from a mentor I had taken classes from in the past. He would help with creating content, as well as with speaking and stage presence. I was really excited to see this because I had a hair show and an online event to speak at in a few months. I contacted him and we began to work the next day.

One of the first things he asked me to do was put my thoughts on a PowerPoint presentation which, technologically speaking, was not exactly within my comfort zone. I had no idea why I needed to do this PowerPoint, or how to do it, but I agreed, then recruited my husband for help as soon as the call ended. By the end of the day, I sent my mentor the first slides so I could get his feedback. Imagine my surprise when he called me shortly after and excitedly said, "You have no idea what you have here! Take slide seven and elaborate, just go to town talking about 'purpose.'" So that's what I did.

My mentor and I spoke every day for the next thirty days, and by the end of our time together I had not only the two presentations ready but six other fifteen-minute talks on self-care, self-love, purpose, empathy, and value. Talk about inspired action! Also, my desire to build a website returned to the forefront and, with it, the image of Amanda, my husband's daughter. I knew she did beautiful work but in the past I had been apprehensive about working with family. What if she didn't like what I was doing? What if we weren't a good fit? Our relationship was top priority and I didn't want anything to come between us. But the thought persisted and I finally reached out to her about doing the website. There were two conditions: I would pay her for her work and she had to be honest with me about my ideas. She agreed and made me promise to tell her if there was something I didn't like.

To tell you this has been wonderful is an understatement. Words can't express the appreciation I have for Amanda, her work, and her support. She is my right-hand person. I could not do this without her. She does my website, my social media posting, my blog posting, mailing list and creates everything I need for my business. I send her content and she brings into being the most beautiful expression of what I'm conveying to reveal my true essence. And, equally as important, she is one of my biggest cheerleaders.

Needless to say, things had taken quite a turn. Instead of spending my six weeks off on tasks to keep busy, I sat at my writing table for twelve to fourteen hours a day, every day, pouring out fifty-eight years of thoughts onto paper. This was so unexpected. In case you haven't noticed, I am an on-the-move kind of person; I am not used to sitting. Yet everything flowed effortlessly, as if this was the work I was always meant to be doing. In six weeks, I was able to get my website up, post weekly on my blog, have content for my talks, and work with Amanda to create a card deck with affirmations. Oh, and I didn't mention I got paid while being off work? Being a business owner I'd never, in forty-plus years, had a day off with pay! So I didn't have to worry about not having income; I could just immerse myself in the joy of creating.

I had never been more in the zone of creating. While many people in the world were struggling with the changes in their world, I was embracing the changes in mine. When I look back, I can see the magic everywhere during this time.

It took my world stopping for me to be quiet enough to hear the nudges from the Universe and surrender to it. I spent each precious day in front of the bedroom window, sitting at Grandma Zimmer's table, settling into the guidance that was flowing freely. All the things I had stressed over and worried about fell into place with grace and ease, and in ways I could not have figured out on my own. It took a pandemic to get my attention. It taught me to get quiet and see where my attention goes.

I start each day with quiet time. I ask for guidance and inspiration. I give thanks for my life and all I have and get to experience. I then open my arms wide and ask to receive all that is for my greatest good. I seldom know what that is, but I am open and I trust while my life unfolds in magical ways.

Be inspired:

The fear that what I wanted to create would not be good enough or accepted held me back from expressing what I have inside. Surrendering to the flow and trusting that everything would come together made the process effortless.

Journal prompt:

Write about a time that you have experienced the unfolding of something unexpected.

Has that changed the way you trust the Universe?

OUT OF HIDING

152

In Closing

"Maybe the journey isn't so much about becoming anything. Maybe it's about unbecoming everything that isn't really you, so you can be who you were meant to be in the first place."

— Paulo Coelho

The Promise

*T*he process of unbecoming everything that isn't me has been my life's work for the last several years. I had piled on layer after layer to hide my true essence; this, in service to my need to feel safe. Turns out it was a false sense of safety. It mostly kept me from expressing who I am and who I want to become. It kept me small and hidden. It kept me isolated from others who I thought wouldn't accept the real me.

I started adding these protective layers when I was a young girl. I had no idea that I was doing it. I only knew that the pain was intense and I didn't like it. If I did something to deflect it and didn't feel it, that meant it was gone, right? I always found a way not to feel the pain I was in. I would keep busy, blame it on someone else, offload it on someone, or simply tell myself that it was stupid to feel like that. Problem is, the pain wasn't really gone. It was hidden behind the outward signs of unhappiness and struggle.

Through this unbecoming I have realized how sensitive I am and have always been. No one taught me how to navigate through this world as a sensitive, empathic person. My parents didn't know. They did what they knew to do, and I learned to do the same.

I have always been able to sense, feel, and know what others are feeling. I have always been able to see someone's intentions behind their actions. It was easy for me to sense when people were lying. I thought that everyone had these experiences, knowings, feelings, and senses. Maybe that's why things were so confusing for me. I could walk into a room and feel or know that something was wrong. I could feel the tension in the air or just somehow knew that something was going on. Time after time, parents or other adults would say that I didn't know what I was talking about, that I was wrong. They would say that nothing was going on, everything was fine. Then I could tell that they weren't telling the truth. Even though I could feel in my body that I was right, I started telling myself that maybe I didn't know what I felt, sensed, or knew. Each time I rejected my truth, I added a layer of denial on top of who I truly was.

Floods of memories surface when I look back on the ways I rejected my essence. I did it in small ways every single day. I did it in big life decisions. The more layers I ever so gently placed over my light, the easier it got to keep adding more. My light became dimmer; I was going deeper and deeper into hiding. There were big life decisions I made KNOWING not to. Everything within me was screaming, "Don't do it!" By that time, though, I was so disconnected from myself that I thought I was wrong. That's what I had been told all my life, so denying my knowing became a way of life. More importantly, that's what I constantly told myself. I no longer trusted my senses or even acknowledged them. I looked outside of myself for everything.

The problem with looking outside myself for all the answers was that I gave my power away to others. My wellbeing was then in someone else's hands, so was my happiness. I told myself that someone else knew what was best for me. I was telling myself that someone else knew me better than I knew myself. This can easily happen when we lose ourselves and forget who we are.

I believe we come into this world fully knowing who we are. We know our value. Our self-worth and self-esteem are in perfect alignment, meaning that our innate value and our *perception* of that value are the same. We are love and we know it. We are a spark of the Divine, a piece of the Universe, a perfect thought of God. As we grow and evolve, we become dependent on others' praise and attention. We start by giving our power away in small ways. As time goes on, we seek more and more approval. We gradually learn to trust others more than the guidance we have inside us. Guidance that is ALWAYS available to us. We are deserving, not because of what we do or don't do. *We are deserving just because we are.*

In my sacred process of "unbecoming," the fierce little girl I denied for so long is emerging. She feels safe to be seen and heard for who she is. She lives every day with a deep connection to her Guidance. We are one, my little girl and me. I believe that the cycle of powerlessness and struggle can be overcome. I believe we can grow and evolve through love instead. I believe that we can break the generational cycles that keep us in pain and keep us passing it on. I believe this because I have done it, and continue to do so.

I believe in you. I promise you that our Guidance quietly waits until we are ready to hear it. No matter how long it takes. Without judgment of us or punishment for denying it, it patiently waits for us. That is Love, and it never changes.

My life is full of magic and miracles, I am blessed beyond measure. I show up every morning by meditating, being open to receive, and being ready to serve. Guidance flows to me all day, every day. As I listen and follow that Guidance, whether it makes sense or not (and sometimes it doesn't), I am shown possibilities and magic. I trust.

Writing this book has been a journey of Guidance, trust, and love. I am elated to share my struggles and breakthroughs and joy with you. It has been the catalyst for me to emerge from hiding and shine my light brightly without apology.

When we change the world changes

With much gratitude and love, I thank you.

If you feel inspired to keep in touch, go to:

Judy-james.com

You will find my latest ventures and offerings.

Sign up for Weekly Wisdom, my weekly newsletter that contains insights, affirmations, journal prompts, and a link to my current blog post.

Leave me a message! I would love to hear from you!

Facebook Page: Judy James

Facebook Group: Judy James Out of Hiding

Instagram: Judyjames.4love

The Wisdom

60 things I've learned in my (almost) 60 years!

These are in no particular order. I am sure that I have forgotten to mention some very important things, but hey, I *am* almost 60!

1. I believe we are all doing the very best we can in every moment. Some moments are better than others, but we are ALL doing the best we can.

2. On the inside, we all long for love and connection, even when our outside says, "Leave me alone."

3. Hurt people hurt people.

4. Our outer world reflects our inner world.

5. I am in charge of my happiness.

6. What I put out into the world, I will receive.

7. I get to choose where I give my power.

8. Your opinion of me is none of my business.

9. Love is the answer.

10. We are never alone.

11. There is a power greater than myself that guides me through this life.

12. Connection is available always and everywhere.

13. When you know better, you do better.

14. Gratitude is life-changing.

15. I set boundaries for what's not okay for me, not to change another person.

16. Money spent on traveling is the best money I ever spent.

17. People's actions and reactions are about them, not me.

18. You are as young as you feel.

19. Having a morning routine that consists of mediation and journaling has changed my life.

20. Always extend grace, for you don't know what someone is going through.

21. Doing the "right" thing doesn't always feel right.

22. Take nothing personally.

23. We ALWAYS have a choice.

24. Everyone we meet mirrors something about ourselves back to us.

25. Everything is "figureoutable."

26. My husband's love has changed my life. Clint, you are my better half. Your mom did good!

27. My family and friends have been my greatest blessings. I love you all!

28. My children have all been my greatest teachers. I love you all!

29. Quiet time every day is a priority.

30. I can't change anyone but me.

31. Everyone has their own journey.

32. I don't know everything.

33. It is a privilege to hear others' stories.

34. I can change the world by changing myself.

35. I am ENOUGH.

36. We are one, no matter our outer appearance or circumstances.

37. Music can change your mood and spark memories in an instant.

38. Being the only girl with five brothers was challenging and held great blessings as well.

39. I LOVE attending live theater performances and music concerts.

40. BEING is more beneficial than doing.

41. I feel the most fulfilled when I'm giving and sharing.

42. One of my favorite and most humbling experiences is to give haircuts at homeless shelters.

43. Death is not final. It's just a transition.

44. There is always more to learn.

45. My thoughts determine how my life goes. (Can you say "micromanage"?)

46. Standing in my power is a choice I make minute by minute.

47. When I'm kind, it's a gift to me too.

48. Anger is deep pain being expressed in the only way we can at that moment.

49. We are meant to thrive, not just survive.

50. There are different ways to look at everything. I will see and experience what I choose to focus on.

51. EVERYTHING happens FOR me.

52. There are more important things than a clean house, like having beloved pets.

53. Gathering people brings me joy.

54. Living free of expectations allows me to experience the peace and magic of letting things unfold in Divine order.

55. My priorities are evident. No matter what I say my priorities are, my actions tell the truth.

56. Learning to be vulnerable has been one of the most difficult and the most rewarding lessons I have learned (am learning).

57. Comparison is absolutely the thief of joy.

58. I feel at home on a beach.

59. Being in nature is healing.

60. The privilege of a lifetime is being who I am. Fully, completely, and authentically who I am.

7 Levels of Why

Have you heard of the 7 levels of 'Why'?

I did this exercise when I was beginning to write this book. I was asked why I wanted to write this book. I really had no idea. It's important for us to know our why. Not just the surface why, but the deep at the core why. This exercise helped me uncover the why that would inspire me to keep going when I wanted to quit. Remembering my why helped me get through the times when I told myself that no one would care about what I had to say and that it wasn't important or helpful to anyone else. It got me to the finish!

Ask yourself a question. This is helpful in providing insight into major things in your life as well as gaining clarity on smaller issues.

It goes like this:

WHY DO I WANT TO WRITE THIS BOOK?

1. So I can put down on paper how I feel.

WHY?

2. So I can release some emotions and heal.

WHY?

3. So I can feel better.

WHY?

4. So I can have more joy in my life.

WHY?

5. So I can live my best life.

WHY?

6. So I can feel free.

WHY?

7. So I don't have to hide any more.

This was an amazing breakthrough moment for me. Being fully me, not hiding who I am is my core Why. Giving myself the freedom to not only express but to share who I am is my life's work. It's what I've always longed for and dreamed of, even though I didn't know it consciously. I have hidden the real me from everyone, including myself. Writing this book has helped me transform my life, giving me the courage to be seen and come 'out of hiding'.

What's your Why?

*"The essence of who we are shines bright when
we allow ourselves to be seen."*

About the Author

$\mathcal{J}$udy James is a wife, mom, grandma, inspirationalist, Reiki Master; Mind, Body, Spirit Practitioner, writer, and speaker. She has also been a hairstylist for forty years.

Judy loves to spend time with family and friends; travel; write; learn; teach and mentor.

Judy started her "Journey Back to Herself" in her late forties when she focused on and prioritized her search for inner peace. She came to realize that lasting peace would come in unexpected ways that didn't always look peaceful on the outside. Her strong connection with Spirit was, and remains, her guiding force.

Judy is a contributing co-author to the 2018 Amazon bestseller, the *52 Weeks of Gratitude Journal.*

Connect with Judy:

Judy-James.com

Judy James FB

Judyjames.4love IG

Acknowledgments

To my husband Clint, your love and support has changed my life. Thank you for believing in me until I could believe in myself. I love and appreciate you!

To Amanda Darr, my bonus daughter, I couldn't have done this without your creative genius and constant support! I love and appreciate you!

To Molly James, my daughter, thank you for your constant support and all the pictures you took of me. I love and appreciate you!

To Sunny Dawn Johnston, my dear friend and mentor, your love, guidance, and support has changed my life! I love and appreciate you!

To my family, thank you for all your support! I love and appreciate you!

To my Fab Five Sisters, your support has been crucial in my growth and expansion. I love and appreciate you all!

To Shanda Trofe, thank you for your gentle guidance and support all the way through this process; you have a way of making it seem effortless. I love and appreciate you!

To my kids: Jennifer, Megan, Molly, and David, thank you for being some of my greatest teachers. I love and appreciate you!

CPSIA information can be obtained
at www.ICGtesting.com
Printed in the USA
LVHW050108170422
716066LV00002B/9